I0424150

THE
JOURNEY
Memoirs of Leeanna Asher

BETTY C. BROWN

PENDIUM

PUBLISHING HOUSE

514-201 Daniels Street
Raleigh, NC 27605

For information, please visit our Web site at
www.pendiumpublishing.com

PENDIUM Publishing and its logo are registered trademarks.

The Journey, Book I
by Betty C. Brown
Copyright © Betty C. Brown, 2008
All Rights Reserved.

ISBN: 0-9724586-5-4

Printed in the United States of America

Without limiting the rights under the copyright reserved above, no part of this publication may be reproduced, stored in or introduced into a retrieval system, or transmitted , in any form, or by any means (electronic, mechanical, photocopying, recording, or otherwise), without the prior written permission of bo th the copyright owner and the above publisher of this book.

PUBLISHER'S NOTE:
Unless otherwise identified, Scripture quotations are taken from the Bible.

BOOKS ARE AVAILABLE AT QUANTITY DISCOUNTS WHEN USED TO PROMOTE PRODUCTS AND SERVICES. FOR INFORMATION PLEASE EMAIL ORDERS@PENDIUMPUBLISHING.COM

If you purchased this book without a cover you should be aware that the book is stolen property. It was reported as "unsold and destroyed" to the publisher and neither the author nor the publisher has received any payment for this "stripped book."

This book is printed on acid-free paper.

To God Be All the Glory

Table of Contents

Preface

The content of this work, I believe, came from God, as He moved me to write this story and the series of books which will follow. There are many good books written about the major characters in our Bibles and from these we are able to discern their humanness as God dealt with them personally and corporately. My book highlights one family out of the thousands of Israelite families, who made that awesome and incredible journey from Egypt, as they walked toward Israel's Promised Land.

The main character telling her family's story and continuing through her children's lives is Leeanna Asher of the tribe of Asher. Leeanna shows the struggles she and many other people endured each miraculous day of their 40 year journey to the border of the Jordan River. They dealt with family life, social life, faith, unbelief, disobedience to God, punishment, awesome miracles, sorrow, despair, death, blessing, birth, hope and much more.

Everyone who has lived life for any amount of years will walk through their own wilderness journey, in the world around us and in the privacy of our own hearts. There is still time to reach the Promised Land our God has promised, no matter what race, creed or color you are, the invitation is wide open to who ever will accept Gods Salvation. As you read this story, please open your mind and place yourself in a pair of shoes that walks, talks, feels, responds, and journeys with the people. Don't sit in your chair and stay detached with human emotions untouched. Come and join the walk and allow your heart to be blessed, refreshed, taught and challenged.

I thank my family for their encouragement and support, especially my sister, Shirlyn.

Betty C Brown

"And they wandered in the wilderness for forty years."

Numbers 14:33

THE
JOURNEY
Memoirs of Leeanna Asher

Chapter 1

My story represents the journey of one family, one among thousands of Israelite families in this wilderness, who were miraculously delivered out of Egypt from slavery and hardships.

This desert journey involved battles with enemies from within and outside of Jacob's descendants. The story focuses on the reality of everyday life and the emotional lives of that congregation. The Bible provides the necessary facts for the reader to gather a well-rounded understanding of the events and individuals highlighted during this journey. This story allows a personal look into the humanity of others and gathers understanding toward how these events affected them.

God Almighty, by His own great mercy, sent Moses into Egypt to procure the Israelites deliverance and to lead us forth from that place with the promise of a land prepared for us, a land full and abundant. We crossed the Red Sea and are three months into our journey to God's Promised Land. My name is Leeanna Asher, and this is where my story begins.

We live a nomadic life where nothing is for sure except the God of our fathers, Who shows us a cloud by day, a fire by night, and awesome miracles. I do not know this miracle working God, but I have the faith passed down to me from the elders. I am awestruck, provided for, and, at the same time, very busy with my life and the everyday duties necessary for survival.

My duties are many and require most of my time. Our belongings are few and have been handed down from our kin. I find that I can and must make do with less than before we started this journey. I am blessed to have the strength to share the load for our household, and to be blessed with little children upon my knees.

"I am grateful, dear God of my fathers, for all Your mighty works toward us."

In a short time, the sun will rise and peek over the land, bringing a sparkle to the sand like little scattered jewels. The manna appears with the dew upon the ground, and the drying dew leaves behind the precious seed we call "manna." It is called manna because no one knew what to call it. Manna means "what is it?" God's miraculous gift of bread from Heaven has not ceased to appear each morning.

Rising from my mat on the soft sand, I consider my duties for the day. First there is the gathering of manna before the sun grows too hot and melts it away. Lifting the flap of the tent entrance, I walked out to start my day. I begin by gently brushing away the sand that had settled the night before on the cloth covering the manna jar.

After a time, I have gathered enough manna, so on returning to the tent, I took down the bowl used for grinding the seeds into bread that feeds and sustains us. Upon hearing me enter, my daughter, Astoria, turns over and looks at me with a lopsided grin on her small face. I whisper to the lovely child.

"Are you hungry, little Astoria?"

She nods her head as curls bounce about her pillow.

"Mama, may I please help with the morning meal today? I know how to grind the miracle seed, I have watched you so carefully, and it is not too hard for me to do."

She leaped up and hugged my legs. Then, she smoothed the wrinkled robe clinging to her little body.

"Oh mama, I want to grow up to be just as strong and pretty as you are and have lots of children to love too."

Astoria took the grinding bowl from my hand and rushed out to the small work area that was just beyond the tent door. She picked up the smooth stone and worked the stone back and forth over the seeds, careful to measure just enough manna into the bowl.

I added more sticks to the smoldering ashes from last night's fire, and soon the hot coals were ready for the pan. The milk left from last night had a yellowish cream covering. Scooping off the cream, I added it to my churning jar and made a mental note that today's work would also include churning butter. Astoria finished her task and beamed at me for the praise she knows I will give her.

Pouring milk in the powdered manna and stirring gently, I pondered over the years ahead when Astoria will have her own house. I poured some of the mixture into the hot cooking pan after adding a small amount of butter. The smell of wafers and honey soon fills the air as each spreading cake begins to bubble and brown. Astoria claps her hands in delight and anticipates the taste of the delicate cake on her tongue.

She mumbles through her first bite of pancake, "All is right with the world isn't it Mama? We can do all things with God can't we?"

"Call your father and brother so they can eat also. Father is beyond that black tent in front of you visiting with his friend, Nathan. Hurry along child so we can get the bowls cleaned and covered. I must go fetch water. You may serve the meal when they arrive."

Picking up the water pot, I hurried to the rock where the water flows in abundance. Our leader, Moses, spoke to the rock by God's command, and water gushed forth before us all. The crowds have already gathered and are discussing this miraculous event.

Miriam and many other women danced and sang with thanksgiving to God for His generous endowment. I longed to be a part of the dancing women, but with my belly extended before me and my time near for this child to be born, I simply clapped my hands and swayed side to side.

"God of my fathers, look down on me, Your handmaiden, and be honored in all Your Majesty, with the simple praise offered from my heart of gratitude."

Remembering the water pot in my arms, I quickly moved past the people to fill my pot. Captivated, I watch the precious liquid flow into the pot. Thoughts begin to swirl in my mind about this life-sustaining liquid. I quickly returned to my tent after speaking a few greetings to a group nearby. My husband and son were coming forth as I arrived. I reached out and ruffled the tawny red hair of our son, Luke. He looked up at me and gave a slight bow of courtesy then ran behind his father to a meeting with the men.

Asher, my husband, spoke to me last eve about the issues the men will be discussing today. "God of my fathers, help them, I pray Thee, to be of one mind and in one accord as they bring these petitions before You. It is written that a three-fold cord is not easily broken. For You, dear God, in Your amazing providence are providing us with the desire to be of one mind. For we are a scattered people and untaught in Your most sacred Law."

I gathered the soiled clothing that needs washing and asked, "Astoria, have you combed your hair today? Bring the comb and ribbon your Grandmother gave you. Sit here and let me help you. There are berries in the front of the small hills. I heard some women speak of it today. As I scrub the clothing, perhaps you and your friends can go there and pick berries. It would be a nice treat for us to enjoy along with the evening meal."

As we made our way to the flowing water, I looked at the clothes in my basket. How could it be? They show no signs of wear and tear? I haven't had to use needle and thread even after scrubbing them clean several times at the rock. This is unusual. The cattle multiply, become fat, and give an abundance of milk. The churn is full and ready for making of curds and butter. We are not cold by night though our clothing is not heavy, and this entire company of people has enough food and some to share. I must tell all these thoughts to my children and repeat them over and over again so they will remember all the good things God has done for us.

So, I picked a place to begin the wash beside a smooth rock that glistened as water splashed against its face. Astoria called to her friend and plans are made to go to the small hills to pick berries. The children skipped away chattering. I busied myself wetting and scrubbing each piece of clothing, and soon the girls were back at my side with a basket of lush berries which we then divided between them.

Most days are the same although the camp moves at the will of the Pillar of Cloud by day or the Pillar of Fire by night. God has given us these constant companions as the visible presence of Himself. When the Pillar lifts up and moves, the entire camp moves in the direction the Pillar goes. When the Pillar settles, the entire camp settles, whether it is for a day or many days. This wonderful guidance is such an awesome sight and very comforting to our people.

I took the butter churn from its place and began the long process of working the plunger up and down. Then, skimming off the cream, I pour off the watery milk left behind, and pour the cream back into the churn, repeating the process over and over again. Soon I will have the precious butter which will be wrapped tightly in cloth and squeezed to remove any remaining water.

Looking up from my work, I see the other women going about their work in a never ending ritual. In the back of our minds are thoughts of the next task to complete before the sun becomes too hot. The wet clothes are spread out to dry on curved wooden stands beside each tent. Most milking of the cattle is done by the men and young boys. Luke mainly stays with his father learning the work of the men and trying to act more grown up than he is.

"Mama, I have washed the berries," Astoria says, as she dries her hands on her robe. "Will you come with me to the place to empty the toilet jar?" she continued, tossing her head in that direction.

As I rise from the work stool, I steady myself on Astoria's

shoulder. This chore requires a walk far enough from camp to bury the contents of the jar.

Everyone has been instructed by God, "When you go to relieve yourself, take a shovel and turn back and cover what has come from you for the Lord our God is Holy and walks among us in the camp."

After completing this duty, Astoria runs quickly ahead of me back to the camp, hoping to have some time to play before helping me with other chores. I wiped the beads of perspiration from my face as I entered the outcrop of the camp. Walking quickly, I sensed a frenzy of excitement among the people. The men have returned from their meeting, and the women and children are scurrying about. Some are wailing and some appear angry. What could all this mean? Is something about to happen? I picked up my pace a little more with hopes that Asher would be by the tent when I arrive so he might inform me of the cause for all this excitement.

Asher watched me approach, and he strides toward me. Taking my arm, he warns me to be more careful while walking in this heat. He comments on the redness of my face and wipes away the moisture with his kerchief.

"My lord," I breathed out in gasps, "tell me please. What is the meaning of the excitement I have witnessed amongst the people? Has there been an accident or a death, or perhaps an ominous sign from God?"

Leading me over to the coolness of the tent, he helped me to sit, poured a cup of cool water, and handed the cup to me. Then, he took a deep breath and began to speak.

My husband struggled to tell me of the matter that had people frantically moving about. Asher is a good, kind man, and a wonderful father to our children. He is wise and has become a mentor for many of the people. Our leader Moses named Asher to be one of the officers over thousands for our Asher Clan. My thoughts are quickly drawn back as I listen to the words Asher is speaking in hushed tones.

"Leeanna, some of the sentries spotted Amalek riders just before dawn close by the foot of Mt. Horeb. Some of our people at the southern end of Israel's encampments have been attacked. Many are hurt and some are dead. "Our great leader, Moses, has called Joshua to choose men and fight Amalek tomorrow. I will be one who goes to this battle and fights for our people, Israel. The God of our fathers will protect and provide for the men going out to battle. Moses, Aaron, and Hur will oversee the battle from the top of the hill. Have faith, dear wife, and pray for Israel, our people. Fear not and remember that God has shown us great and mighty things these last three months. It is for sure that He will not abandon His people, Israel, now!"

I sat stunned, my eyes filling with tears. This is something I nor Israel has ever faced. We have seen cruelty and slavery in Egypt, but God delivered us from all that. Is this happening to us because so many have mumbled and are dissatisfied since we were brought out from Egypt? Asher seemed to read my thoughts. He reached out, pulled me up from my stool, and gently folded his arms about me.

"Leeanna," he whispered choking back tears, "I am counting on your strength to give me comfort in mind and heart so that I won't be overly concerned about you and the children. Then I can go with peace of mind to perform my duties alongside our people. I cannot help but worry for your safety, but all of us must do our part so we can become the one nation that the God of our fathers called us to be. You will have the children to help you gather the morning manna and quails in the evening. The water from the rock is still flowing abundantly. The older men, who do not go out to battle, have been given their duties to help the women and children in whatever manner they need. With God's good mercy upon us, this battle will be won, and the men will return from the battle before the sun goes down," Asher said, looking into my eyes for assurance.

"Of course, beloved, I am confident of Israel's success. My heart and prayers for you and Israel are even now ascending to our benevolent God for the safety of all Israel. It is written that we must love and serve the Lord our God with all our heart, strength, and mind. If this battle is His will, then we must be prepared to sacrifice all for the Savior of our people," I assured him, placing a hand against his cheek.

With the men gone, the day is busy, but I am constantly watching the hills in hopes that some miraculous intervention has taken place, and the battle would not be fought. Luke and Astoria are helping to gather the wonderful white seed that looks like hoar frost lying on top of the ground. This miracle bread sent down from God in heaven has not failed to appear every morning for our daily bread as He promised Moses. My family loves to gather the precious seed each morning while visiting with friends. When baked, it has the taste of wafers and honey.

Last night's tearful farewells between the children and their father have all been forgotten as they chatter and gather our daily portion of manna. I have noticed that no matter how much manna we gather or how little, it is always enough.

"God Almighty, filled with mercy and kindness, by Your own hand, You have brought this to be, and, by Your wisdom, everyone has plenty. I know You are taking great care of the men of Israel just as You uphold us all with Your right hand. I wish no one any harm, but neither do I want my people to suffer at the hands of Amalek. I bless and thank You for the wonderful kindness shown to us," I prayed with gratitude.

Asher was kind enough yesterday to gather wood for the morning fire. The coals from last night's fire are still smoking, so I placed more chips on them for baking the bread. I think today we will have some of the new butter with these loaves and fresh warm milk to top off the meal. My husband doesn't have a large number in his herd, so it wasn't long before Mathius, our dear old friend, had milked the herd and brought the milk to me.

Noticing the twinkle in his blue eyes as he watched the loaves baking, I quickly made room for him to sit at the meal with us. Helping us with the milking left no time for him to gather manna for himself. So after we completed our meal, I took a piece of cloth, wrapped it around the other loaf with a generous helping of butter, and gave it to him with all my gratitude for his help.

"I am sending Luke along with you to assist in drawing and carrying water for the animals, Mathius," I said.

He took the loaf from my hand and bowed a courteous 'thank you' in return. "May the smile of God be upon thee this day, and may His blessed hand be upon our people, Israel," he prayed as he turned to leave.

"Amen and amen," was my sincere reply.

Just after they left to fetch water for the herd, I reached down to collect the bowls we had eaten from. A sharp pain grasped my side and traveled across and down my body to the other side.

"My God help, I pray thee, Your handmaid this day."

Making my way across the short distance to Jillian's tent, I am racked again with a stabbing pain. My body is wet with perspiration, and my knees are threatening to fold. The smell of baking bread permeates the air. Normally it is welcome and pleasant, but I feel waves of nausea sweeping up within me. Managing to gather enough air in my lungs to speak, I call out with hope that someone will hear me and come. As another pain plunges through my body, the weakness is more than I can take. Trying desperately to stand up on weakened legs, I reach for the nearest tent pole for support and ease my tortured body down to the ground. Reaching for a stick, I strike on the clay jar near me trying to make enough noise for Jillian to hear.

I faintly hear the feminine voice speaking softly but confidently at my shoulder, urging me to lean on her as she presses against my waist leading me inside the tent. Soon there are more voices, and the small shelter has become teamed with activity. Someone begins to remove my sweat soaked robe, and immediately I sense a slight coolness of air against my skin. The pain is causing my body to bend forward, but there are hands under my arms supporting me as I am gently lowered down onto the birthing stool. Moist towels are passed over my face and neck giving small amounts of cool relief, and another towel is placed between my teeth. Pressed hard against my palms, the handles of the birthing stool are a welcome grasp for my trembling hands.

"Do not worry where your children are. Michelle has gone to fetch them and will keep them with her until this child has been born," whispered Jillian. "The mountain you are climbing at this time is more than enough effort spent. The child in your womb has shown clearly that he waits for no man, and, sadly, your dear husband is not with you. But what a time of joy will be had when he returns to find there are four of you waiting for him where he had left only three."

"My dear friend, I am so grateful for the kind and generous help from all these women. Surely we share kindred spirits in our plights of life. So much befalls us as we are swept along on the path we are destined to walk. And who but the good Lord of glory knows the heartache and pain we endure, yet gives us such pleasure to watch our little ones born, grow, marry, and have children of their own. Even with the pain, heartache, suffering, fear and joy that goes with it."

Suddenly there is a swoosh of water as the next pain causes my breath to catch. I know from experience it will not be long now before my baby enters this world with ringing cries mingled with the rejoicing of my friends in prayers and thanksgiving to the God of our fathers. I must try to concentrate on the task at hand so I can work with the pain and not against it. The baby needs my fullest attention to help him escape from his tiny chamber and into this world God created for us.

My labor has continued for such a long time.

"Oh Merciful God, I beseech Thee. Please bring a quick end to these pains of birth and help my child to arrive soon."

My body has grown weak, and I struggle to hold the handles of this stool. There are flickers of light before my eyes like when the night fire looses its tiny cinders to fly into the star-filled sky. The dryness in my throat from muffled screams is matched only by the dryness of my eyes where tears had flowed so quietly before.

"If there is something wrong with the child, I pray that You will help him to overcome the torture of this birth and lead him safely through into Jillian's waiting hands."

Now, I am being lifted and placed on a mat. I can hear the soft crunch of straw beneath me. Jillian is instructing me to trust her and hold tightly to the poles on each side of me. She says the baby needs to be turned because he is not in the correct position for birth, and there isn't much time. I feel strong hands grasp my shoulders and legs as a fiery hot pain sears through my lower belly causing me to scream out from the depth of my soul. My body is racked with convulsive waves of pain as Jillian turns the baby inside of me.

"This child is a big one, Leeanna. He is turned now so he can come forth to see his mother!" Jillian said.

The urge to push overwhelms me, and I hear the persuasive voice of my friend coaching me on. Almost immediately, I hear the wailing cry of my baby as he burst forth to his waiting audience.

"Welcome to the world, little Andrew Ben Asher! Soon I will have you cleaned up so you may meet your mother!" Jillian squealed with joy amid the praises and prayers of the other women. "What a great affair your entrance has caused, and throughout your life may you be as aggressive as you were this day!"

It seems I am looking into the eyes of my husband as I watch our son snuggle against my breast. Andrew Ben Asher was the name chosen for this child by my father-in-law, Johan Ben Asher, almost from the time of conception. Tucking this precious bundle into the swaddling cloth, I close my weary eyes for a moment of blissful rest.

I am awakened from my pleasant rest by a flurry of hushed whispers. Adjusting my sore eyes to the faint light of an oil lamp, I see the flap of the tent entrance is turned back against the outside. A gentle breeze allows the flame to dance back and forth. The movement near my breast jolts my memory as to what has taken place. Lifting my arm across my chest is quite a struggle, but I manage to uncover the tiny bundle nestled at my side.

"God be praised," I whisper aloud. "What a breech you made in the day's work planned while your father is away in battle. And you, little Andrew, decided on your own to separate me from my plans and have, by your birth this day, enlightened me that God's will be done. Our thoughts are not His thoughts neither are our ways His ways. I thank You, blessed Lord God Almighty, for the gift of this child and for showing great mercy to me through this time of travail," I prayed with all my heart.

"Leeanna, have you come back to us from your rest and discovered a treasure snuggled in your embrace?" Jillian called out to me. "He is, for certain, a beautiful baby, and I thank God that the two of you pulled through this event without harm. We were worried for a while about the outcome of his birth. You, my dear, have lost much blood, and your body is weak. It is our decision that you remain here with me until you are stronger so I can watch over you and the child. As soon as the other women come back, we will help you move around and change your dressings."

    The baby made a sound like a little kitten, letting me know that he is hungry. Jillian assisted me in placing his tiny mouth to my breast. As he begins to suckle, my heart is flooded with love for this innocent baby. The joy I feel at this precious moment, seeing the cycle of life begin once again, can only be experienced by a woman and cannot be attested to by mere words.

    "Yes, dear Lord, in Your benevolence. You have ordained such joy for the woman to experience. Only You can take great pain and bring something so good from it. Your words to the woman was that You would multiply the conception of children and increase the pain of birth, but Almighty God, You knew the reward of this command would make it worth all the pain we endure. Children are a gift from the Lord and as arrows in a man's hand. Happy is the man who has his quiver full of these arrows."

    "Has she awakened?" asked Hanna from the tent door. "We have come to help change and dress her in a fresh gown," she continued, showing a bundle of white cloth in her arms. "Yes, you are awake, little mother! You gave us all a scare earlier. This birth had generated quite a stir about the camp. Even now, old Mathias had claimed the place by the tent entrance, sitting with churn and dasher, making curds for your family table."

    Hanna and the other woman chattered continuously as they cleaned and dressed me in the fresh gown.

    Suddenly I hear sounds of a crowd running with shouts of rejoicing filling the air. Jillian hurries to the tent door and bent her head toward Matthias in order to determine what the matter is. I pushed myself up from the mat as anxiety fills my heart. Catching glimpses of people as they rush past the door, my fear mounts. The other women quickly join Jillian at the front entrance, and I am temporarily forgotten. What has happened to cause such a commotion? Jillian finally turns back toward me. Seeing the fear on my face, she rushes to me and places her hand on my arm, gently laying me back on the mat again.

    "Leeanna," she gasped, "the men of Israel are returning to camp. The battle with Amalek is over. There is news from a runner that some of our men are injured and regrettably a few are dead. There have been no names reported as to who these men are, so we all must wait and continue to pray. You are not able to go out with the other women of the camp to meet your husband, so Matthias is even now making his way to meet him in your stead."

    "Oh God of our Israel, I beg You please for the lives of the wounded and comfort those who have lost loved ones. There is rejoicing in the camp over the returning men, and I pray that the battle has brought our enemies to an end. Though death is not a thing to be celebrated, we lifted our swords against no man until we were provoked by Amalek in the camps of Your people, Israel. Grant Your people grace not to shrink back in times to come because of the lives lost this day. Protect us, I pray, and give us strength to continue forward on our journey to the place where we will be safely planted forever," I prayed aloud.

Jillian's trembling lips echo, "Amen and amen."

The baby at my side stirs and begins to cry loudly. Jillian stoops down and picks him up, cradling him against her chest.

"Oh, so you want to join in the rejoicing with those outside these walls of skin, do you little Andrew?" she coos against his reddening face as he continues to cry with more volume.

Swaying back and forth, she ministers soothing words of comfort and gently pats the baby's back. A burp from the tiny bundle is heard, and slowly he begins to rest from his outburst.

"Do I hear the voice of my son shattering my eardrums and announcing his father's arrival?" Asher shouts from just beyond the tent entrance. "By the grace of God, I have come back to such a welcome as this. My newborn son sings along with all Israel before I have had the chance to be properly introduced to him myself," laughs my husband as he strides into the dimness of the tent.

Jillian turns and lays the baby in Asher's outstretched arms. Tears of happiness run down his ruddy cheeks as he receives his son and looks down into Andrew's face. The scene before me makes my heart flutter with happiness. My Asher has returned home safely and is stroking the head of his newborn son. I feel a lump in my throat at the sight taking place before me. Beyond all doubt, there most assuredly is a God, and He provided for us this wonderful time of reunion and bliss.

Asher gently lays the baby beside me with such love in his eyes. He reaches for my hand, pressing it to his lips. Jillian softly walks out from the tent to allow us some time alone. Hopefully her husband is waiting for her beyond the door, and, with searching eyes, I look into Asher's face as I inquire about the well being of Jillian's husband.

"I have no knowledge of Seraymas Ben Asher, but our company of men sustained only a few injuries. I am sure he faired well. There were some men of Israel who lay down their lives today for our just cause, but the day has grown almost to an end. So on the morrow, all the men will gather before our leader with full reports. Even so my dear wife, I must leave you and our son for just a while longer to go throughout the Asher campsites. I must determine the fate of each man and what concerns need to be addressed for assistance."

He brushed my forehead with a kiss.

Reluctantly, Asher turns to leave just as Jillian steps back into the room. He bows before her and expresses gratitude for her charity to his family. Jillian takes the opportunity to recite the information of my labor and Andrew's birth. I watch as Asher's head drops down and moves from side to side as he listens to the account. They walked outside together as she continued her report.

Asher stood before the entrance, and his shoulders begin to shake with sobbing. Jillian placed her hand upon his arm and nodded her head as if in agreement with some plan. After a few moments, she returns to my side and begins preparing the baby and me for the evening.

"You have had a very long and laborious day, my dear. I have Asher's consent for you to remain here for the evening so I can watch over you and help with the child. He has gone first to his own dwelling to greet your other two children and sit at meat with them before going out to visit the Asher camps," Jillian announces. "Soon, Hanna will bring food Matthias prepared for us, while he awaited the birth of the child. The camps are in a flurry of excitement, and it will require quite a spell of Asher's time before he comes again to your dwelling. I pray that you will agree with this arrangement."

My thoughts reel in my head as though I have spun around and around as I did when I was only a child. The flickering of the lamp mixed with shadows dancing against the tent walls are creating a lullaby leading me into a gentle sleep. I sense no hunger for food or any more excitement this day. Sliding into a peaceful rest with happy thoughts of the safety of family and friends is enough.

"Bless You my God, for all that You have done. May the thoughts and the meditations of my heart be acceptable in Your eyes, dear Lord of Glory! Amen."

****

Chapter 2

What exciting news! Moses, our leader, has been commanded by God to have all the people cleanse and sanctify themselves. For in three days God is going to speak to the whole congregation from the mountain top. We are to bathe and wash our clothes, and the men are not to have relations with their wives for three days. And be sure, Moses warned us, not to go near the foot of the mountain. Neither go up on it lest we die. There is so much to do while preparing for this glorious event, and I am thankful my strength has returned since the birth of my child, Andrew.

Asher and I spent much time last eve discussing the concerns of what such an event would call for in regards to each individual in this camp and the responsibility for our own hearts' preparation. Our people have longed for hundreds of years to see, hear, and be partakers of what our forefathers experienced with God. Such preparation cannot be taken unwisely or without searching within our own selves to see what uncleanness and roots of evil are embedded there. What a fearful and yet awesome affair all of this will be!

Andrew awakens and startles me from my thoughts. This little baby unfortunately won't know or remember this glorious encounter of listening to God. I will be faithful to rehearse in the ears of my children all the great and mighty things God has done for His people, Israel.

As I watch the baby suckle, I journeyed into my own heart where weeds have grown for far too long. It may take years or a lifetime to forget the miseries that our people endured at the hands of the Egyptian people. It may be that the blessing of deliverance from that place includes the memory of what was and is evil when people forget or ignore God. It is possible that such disdainful pearls of wisdom will help us to remember the past and will give us understanding toward our future choices in life. Forgiveness is an action taught to us from our fathers, but forgiveness must be sought and experienced continually within one's own heart until that good seed has taken root.

When I was a child, my father called his children to him, while standing by the family's tiny garden, to demonstrate the lesson on forgiveness. As we stood looking at father, he instructed our eyes down toward the earth with a gesture of his hand. Stooping down with his knees resting upon the hard soil before him, he began to speak.

"Do you see the hard resistant soil before you here?" asked father, "And do you pay attention to how low I must place myself to the soil to test its resistance?"

"This soil is like my resistant heart, and being low to the soil represents my will to test my heart before God. Now that I have inspected the soil at close level, I am able to determine what must be done to prepare the soil before it will bring forth fruit. In the same way, God helps me to look at all the different wrongs in my heart and helps me determine what must be done to correct them so my heart will be fruitful."

"The plow I hold in my hand will break up the hard soil, and it takes a lot of my strength and the ability to use it. So in like manner, this plow is like the word of God. It is sharp as a two-edged sword and will break up the hard places in my heart. But my strength and ability are needed to cooperate with God's word in allowing it to do its work in me."

"When God's word has found a place in my heart that needs softening up, it is up to me to give that place over to Him or to let that place lay fallow and unusable. Whenever I make the choice in my heart to hold hard feelings against another for whatever reason, that I feel my anger or pride is justified, then that place becomes barren. Soon all manner of weeds spring up in it and choke at the places I had previously planted with good seed. The seed, being my obedience and progress in my walk with God, needs nourishment, watering, watching over, and mercy from Him Who makes the seed grow. If I want all of these things to prosper in my heart and life, then I must learn to give the same consideration where others are concerned. Growing and tending a garden is not an easy task just as growing my heart up in God's word, at times, is not easy. But continuous obedience and attention to His word will, indeed, work in my heart a fruitful life. Therefore, if you want forgiveness from God for your shortcomings, then allow Him to help plow up your heart. And "you" must plant that small seed, and let it grow, unencumbered and fruitful, so that you will have like kind to share with others. Remember, my children, that it is the little foxes that destroy the vines."

After finishing his demonstration, he dismissed us to go and play.

Little Andrew sleeps peacefully against my breast as I reminisce about my father's clear demonstration to his children. Father passed on one month before Moses came to Egypt to bring God's people out. Of course, our extended families of Israelites are camped all around me, but the closeness of my own father cannot be replaced.

His insight in the words and ways of God were treasures that our close family gathered like we gather the manna each morning for the day's bread.

Reluctantly, I rise up and place the baby on my pallet, tucking his little hands beside him. There are many things I need to tell my own children concerning what I learned from both my parents, and I think tonight after the meal would be a good time to begin. Father was faithful to pass on to his children the wisdom he gleaned from speaking tirelessly to the elders and putting these principles into action in his life.

He greatly loved and reverenced God and learned that the fear of the Lord is the beginning of wisdom for us all.

****

"Will you please hold still Astoria?" I pleaded while trying to rinse her hair.

Realizing the request was being drowned out from the water running over her ears, I quickly finish the task and wind a clean cloth over her long wet hair. Motioning for Luke to take his turn, I attempt to wash his hair, rubbing vigorously.

Astoria watches the entire scene with a far away look on her pretty face. Realizing she has something on her mind, I ask what the matter could be. With a puzzled look, she attempts to tell me as I try to restrain Luke's wiggles beneath my hands.

"I am so sorry Astoria." I blurted out in gasps. "Could you please pass the pitcher of water to finish Luke's hair before I have to swat his behind? I am already wet from my shoulders to my knees from both of you twisting about as your hair was washed. I promise you when I am done here, I will sit down and listen to what you tried to say."

After toweling Luke's hair, I warned him not to be rolling on the ground getting dirty, so I don't have to do this all over again.

"Mama, could I please go find father?" Luke asked as he brushes back the straggles of hair from his face. "I promise to be careful, and will try very hard not to get dirty while looking for him."

With a nod of my head, Luke rushes off to find Asher, relieved, I am sure, to escape from the torment he had just endured.

Turning my attention to cleaning up the bowls from their hair washings, I temporarily forgot Astoria. Hearing a big sigh from behind my back, I turned about in time to see Astoria brush tears from her face.

"Little lamb, what is the meaning of your tears. I only would have been a few moments cleaning the bowls and then would have sat and listened. Please tell me, what is the affliction upon your little heart, child?" I asked, sitting down beside her.

"Mama, I am so small when standing beside other children my age. They laugh at me when I am not able to reach or jump high like they can. Tandra pulled on my arms to see if they would grow out longer, and when I still couldn't reach high, the other girls laughed. They say I am of no use when we play games because I am too scared to turn flips and climb on big rocks. Why can't I be more like Luke and his friends? I watch them roll and climb and wrestle everyday, they have so much fun. Inside is a feeling of anger and jealousy as I watch them play, and I wonder why I can't do the things I see others do. Mama, will I grow up to be of use to anyone, or will I stay the way I am and become lonely with no friends?"

With great tenderness, I pull my daughter to my breast, smooth back her hair, and plant kisses on top of her little head. My heart feels as if it is breaking for this precious child. I sensed a thunderous voice well up from deep within my soul to bring peace to her heart with the words of God which have helped me throughout dry places in my life. My father spent most all his breath rehearsing the lessons we needed to hear and learn for our trip through this life. He took every opportunity, in all circumstances, to teach us about God and His word and the ability to live life to the fullest with simple everyday lessons.

"Oh dear God, my own daughter, my flesh and blood child, needs some words of wisdom in a way her little heart can understand. Please help me, with words from your heart to mine, to bathe her in encouragement as my father always did for me. In her eyes and innocence, she cannot see past her pain at this time. Please flood me with your wisdom so I can apply the healing ointment to her heart and mind. Thank You," I prayed as I rocked her in my lap.

"Little lamb, there is so much more to life and people other than being able to reach or climb. You might not see that now, but God has a beautiful place and plan for you. He knows what is in your heart, all the cares, fears, and feelings of helplessness that you have. God made you in my womb, and He planned for your weakness and strength in life. Though you are but a child now, you will grow into a great woman in

God's eyes. There are many different people, and we all have a path to follow. No one person has the same path or plan in His eyes. God will use each one to complete His plan as they walk through their lives. He will also use you according to His plan. If you look at the sand on your toes, you can tell that each grain of sand is different. Yet the sand is not bothered by this. It accepts the difference. Your father molds pitchers and bowls from clay for different uses. We know there is a difference for each one's use, but we are not bothered by it. The birds in the heavens are all different and sing songs of joy to fill our ears, but we don't mind that they are different because we enjoy the beauty and melody of each one. The girls you play with are all different. Each one of them has talents, strengths and weaknesses. You know who called your name by the sound of their voice because each girl has a different voice. When you think on these things, would you fault your friends because they are not just the same as you? Of course you wouldn't. As each one grows into a young woman, you will learn to appreciate the differences. God knows your heart, Astoria, and He will use you in a way as to bring glory and honor to His name with the talents He has given to you. He will use you to bring encouragement and blessing to whomever He brings across your path. God will use those weaknesses that you have and turn them into strength to guide you and others in life. Do you understand all this, dear?" I asked, while softly stroking her hair.

Even before I had finished speaking, I could feel her shoulders relax against me. She looked up with a tear stained face and smiled sweetly, nodding her head as she wrapped her arms around my neck.

"Mama, I could see a picture of everything as you talked about it. My mind was full of beautiful images, and my chest feels full of love. I enjoyed the different pictures you painted inside of my head, and I don't feel hurt in my heart anymore."

Giving her a big hug, I told her that when I was a child and my father talked to me this way, that's the way I felt, too. We sat and chatted for a time, and her face returned to the happy Astoria.

Looking out across the maze of tents, I noticed the sky growing gray with the approach of evening. Soon Asher and Luke would be along with quail for the evening meal. Tomorrow will be a great and memorable day for us all. We will meet God from His position on the mountain. Everyone around us has been preparing for this event. I cannot explain how I feel about the day to come, but I have searched my heart and asked God's mercy upon me in the things I might have missed in this search. As far as I know, we will be prepared to go before God and hear His words when Moses calls us out in the morning.

Busying myself with the preparations for dinner, I began singing a song from long ago that was taught to me as a child. There is peace in my heart and peace with my family. I could not have known the havoc that tomorrow would bring.

****

The day is breaking, and the sound of thunder fills the tent. Clearing my mind from sleep, I quickly rise up and awake the children sleeping nearby. Asher has already gone out to collect the morning manna. The children struggle forth from beneath their covers as I pick up the baby for nursing. Reminding them of today's glorious plan, they quickly begin asking more questions than I can answer. Luke scurries out the door in search of Asher, and Astoria helps me change and bathe Andrew.

The thundering makes me uneasy. Pulling back the door flap, I looked out into the sky. I saw others standing about looking up, too. Closing the flap, I returned to Andrew to suckle him from my breast. Soon Asher and Luke will return and I won't be as nervous. For now, I concentrate on the sweet face of the baby enjoying his milk.

Asher returned just as I finished feeding Andrew.

"Moses has called all the people to come out and congregate before the mountain," he announces as he enters the tent, setting the manna pot to one side. "I have come to fetch you and the children. Luke is waiting for us with Mathias. Are you ready to go forth and meet the Lord our God?" He twirled me around the tent while Astoria giggled and danced with us. "I have waited for such a day as this, to meet the God of our fathers and to see with my own eyes the glory of His presence. We shall all stand together before Him as a family of Asher. God be praised for His enduring grace upon this family."

"Asher, what is the meaning of that thunder?" I questioned my happy husband.

"Leeanna, the sounds of thunder and flashes of lightening are coming from Mount Sinai. This is a symbol of God's presence upon the mountain. There are dark clouds, the mountain is quaking, and the sound of a trumpet grows louder. Come, we must hurry. You carry Andrew, and I will hold Astoria's hand. Mathias will hold Luke's hand. Are we ready now to go?" he asked as I retrieved Andrew from the mat and wrapped him in a blanket.

"Yes indeed, we are ready. May this day be blessed and in our memories for ever and ever!" I replied as we walked out into the morning.

Chapter 3

Luke began jumping up and down, clapping his hands, as we joined him and Mathias. Astoria pulled free from her father's grasp and rushed to Luke, joining him in jumping and clapping. Mathias said something as he bowed in courtesy before us, but I couldn't understand him because of the children. Moving closer to Mathias, I placed my free hand upon his shoulder, bent low, and asked him to repeat his words. As Mathias sees the baby's face, he lifts the edge of the blanket with his weathered hands and peers into Andrew's tiny face. He turns slightly, points toward the mountain, and drops his head forward. I realize he is showing God the face of this child and is showing Andrew the mountain we will gather before to give thanks to the Mighty One.

What an awesome and frightening site to behold! I can't help but stare at the mountain with the dark clouds atop and thundering and lightening filling the space above it. We continued walking past all the tents on this side of the camp to get a clear area at the base of the mountain. I am constantly stumbling because I can't stop looking at this awesome site. Fear is trying to take over my mind and body as we draw closer and closer to the clearing. Asher put his arm about my shoulders. I looked up at him and found that he was carrying Astoria snuggled close to his chest.

The trumpet grows louder and louder, the mountain quakes, and brings a shaking to the earth beneath our feet. Judging the size of the crowd before us, it looks as though everyone from camp has gathered. Stopping in a clearing behind the crowd, we take a few moments to look around at the assembly of Israel. Almost everyone gathered here are from our people, Israel, having sprung from the loins of our forefather, Jacob. To try to number the lot of us would, indeed, be a great task.

The God of our forefathers, Abraham, Isaac, and Jacob, has remained true to His promise, that He would make a mighty nation from them. All eyes are on the mountain, and the sounds of fear are heard from those around me. I realize that Asher is also frightened. I feel his trembling hand upon my shoulder. Luke is standing next to Asher on the left side of Mathias. He grasps his father's tunic while holding tightly to Mathias.

The trumpet is getting so loud that people are starting to shrink back further. Asher and I step aside to allow people past us. We are forced to continually step back so that soon the space ahead of us has less people than before. Asher lifts his hand from my shoulder and points toward the mountain. Moses is standing just before it with his arms upraised with a staff in one hand. The crowd grows suddenly silent, and all the sounds from the mountain decrease at once.

Moses speaks out, his voice ringing clearly in our ears.

"Speak, oh blessed God of Israel, for thy people are now gathered and wait before You to hear Your voice and to give heed to Your words this glorious day! What awesome demonstrations You have shown us from the day of our departure from Egypt until now. We have waited to assemble before Your mighty presence to affirm the ways of worship that You desire."

Immediately, a glorious, heavenly voice, like none I have ever heard, comes forth, and the sound of this voice is as if it were all around and inside us. Surely, this voice can be none other than the voice of God speaking to all of us. The Voice commands Moses to come up to the top of the mountain.

Moses leaves his post at the foot of the mountain and quickly begins the assent. The fire and smoke from atop the mountain have not stopped. All the people watch in pure fright as our leader disappears within the cloud of smoke.

Now that Moses has gone up the mountain, the people begin to weep as feelings of fear become prevalent among us all. Children are clutching parents and sobbing. Their cries are mingled with many of their parents' tears as we try to make understanding of what this means.

Why did God not speak to us, and why was it that Moses had to return to the mountain top at this time? Is God so displeased with us that He will not fulfill His own command to us, to gather here, and He would speak? The murmurs of the crowd grow as more people shrink further back from the immediate area of the mountain.

Turning toward my husband, I see tears sliding down his cheeks. He bends to put Astoria down on her feet but slips to his knees after depositing her in front of us. He covers his face with his hands, and his shoulders begin shaking with sobs like one that appears to be heart broken. Motioning for Mathias to take the baby from my arms, I slip down beside Asher and place my arm about his waist. The prayer coming from his heart erupts as each word spoken makes an agonizing, mournful sound. Astoria and Luke covered our backs with their little bodies, and laid their heads on our shoulders as a gesture of their concern.

Much time passed, before someone announced in a flurry of excitement that Moses was seen descending the mountain. Again, the loudness of the crowd assuaged into low murmurs until Moses took his position where he stood previously. As Moses lifts his arms and staff toward the sky, the crowd is completely silent.

The quaking ground beneath our feet causes Moses' voice to quiver as he speaks a message to us. He reminds the people not to come up on the mountain or too near the base of it. No one should try to break through to gaze at the Lord lest God break forth upon them and kill them. A tremendous gasp is heard circulating the entire congregation and a frenzied movement backwards begins again. When all movement has stopped, God's voice clearly and plainly begins to speak again.

And God spoke all these words saying, "I am the Lord thy God, which has brought you out of the land of Egypt, out of the house of bondage. You shall have no other gods before Me. You shall not make any graven image, or any likeness of any thing that is in heaven above, or that is in the earth beneath, or that is in the water under the earth. You shall not bow down yourself to them, nor serve them, for I am a jealous God, visiting the iniquity of the fathers upon the children unto the third and forth generation of them that hate Me and showing mercy to thousands of them that love me and keep my commandments."

"You shall not take the name of the Lord your God in vain; for the Lord will not hold him guiltless that takes His name in vain."

"Remember the Sabbath day, to keep it holy. Six days shall you labor, and do all your work; but the seventh day is the Sabbath of the Lord your God; in it you shall not do any work, you nor your son, nor your daughter, your manservant, nor maidservant, nor your cattle, nor your stranger that is within your house: for in six days the Lord made heaven and earth, the sea, and all that is in them, and rested the seventh day; therefore the Lord blessed the seventh day, and made it holy. "

"Honor your father and your mother, that your days may be long upon the land that the Lord your God gives you."

"You shall not kill; you shall not commit adultery; you shall not steal; you shall not bear false witness against your neighbor. You shall not covet your neighbor's house, his wife, his manservant, his maidservant, his animals, or anything that is your neighbors."

All the people heard the thundering, saw the lightening, heard the noise of the trumpet, and saw the mountain smoking. When the people saw it, they moved from their places and stood far off.

As more time passed, some men had an opportunity to communicate to Moses saying, "You speak to us and we will listen, but let not God speak to us lest we die."

The sights and happenings of this day had taken a fearful hold on the hearts and minds of the people; everyone thought that we would surely die.

Moses answered their shouts saying, "Do not be afraid, for God has come to prove you that His worship may be before your faces and that you may not sin. God has this day talked with you from heaven." But the people continued to stand afar off, so Moses went near to the thick darkness where God was.

We all stood there, not knowing what to do after hearing these words. After a long time, most everyone began wandering back to camp. No one had eaten, and the children were getting fussy. So not knowing what else would take place, we also returned to the camp. I felt overcome with emotions. Somehow, my feelings were of sadness and sorrow mixed with joy. My mind was a whirl of thoughts. My heart was telling me that something just wasn't right, though I couldn't grasp the reason. As we walked along toward the tent, Asher continuously looked back over his shoulder toward the mountain, an awesome, brilliant sight in the midst of the day. There wasn't much conversation between us on the walk, and the children were quiet. Mathias continued to wipe his eyes at times. There was more of a bounce to his step, and his face had a look of peace.

After the meal was prepared and eaten, messengers came from Moses. All the people were to gather so he could rehearse in our ears all the things God had spoken to him. Everyone quickly assembled and watched as Moses approached and stood before us. He began proclaiming all the words and ordinances God had given to him.

All the people answered Moses with one voice and said, "Everything which the Lord has said, we will do."

During the night, Moses wrote everything God had said in a book. He rose up early in the morning, and built an altar at the foot of the mountain and twelve pillars, according to the twelve tribes of Israel. He sent young men to offer sacrifices on the altar to the Lord. He again stood before the people and read all the words of the Lord written in the book of the covenant.

Again all the people said, "All the Lord has said, we will obey and do."

So Moses took some of the blood of the sacrifices and sprinkled it on the people.

"This is the blood of the covenant which the Lord made with you concerning all these words."

Then Moses, Aaron, Nadab, Abihu, and seventy of the elders of Israel went up into the mountain. The dark clouds were upon the mountain of Sinai for many days.

****

Seven days have passed since gathering at the mountain to hear God's spoken word. Neither Asher nor the children have said much concerning that day, and the camps about us seem to be in a similar mood. Normal conversation has been kept at a lower volume, and there is not as much visiting among the people as there was before. Everyone goes about their daily chores as usual but with an air of solitude, as if their hearts are burdened. The children have finally gone out to play with friends, and some sounds of normalcy are returning with their chattering and laughing about the camps.

When Asher returned from the milking and sat down to eat, I watched his face for the right time to question him concerning his thoughts.

"Asher, there are some thoughts in my heart concerning the day the people gathered at the mountain," I said, while looking for a sign of acceptance.

"Say on, Leeanna," was his reply.

Gathering courage from his reply, I began my quest to determine how that day had affected him. Leaning closer to his sitting position, I reached to take his hand. He smiled and made motion with a nod of his head that he was willing to hear me.

"As we stood before the mountain that day," I said, "God spoke telling Moses to come back up the mountain. What were your thoughts as we stood and watched? If it is not your will to talk about it, perhaps at some other time you might tell me." He dropped his chin toward his chest.

Slowly raising his eyes, the glisten of tears visible, he shook his head, assuring me that he would tell me now.

"I had waited for a long time to receive any direct communication from God." he explained, pulling the words from his heart. "When God called Moses to come to the top of the mountain and had not spoken to the assembly below, I felt that perhaps He was not going to speak after all. I felt as though I was not worthy to stand before such an awesome God and be eligible to hear His precious words. My knees became weak and began to buckle beneath me as I attempted to set Astoria on her feet. I had built up such excitement about that day, and then I thought that God wasn't going to speak to us. So from my anguished heart, my words spilled out to Him. I felt my heart break as I pleaded and begged forgiveness for all that I was guilty of, and also for the whole assembly surrounding me. As I prayed and released my heart to Him, I began to sense a flood of relief and assurance that He had heard me and that He loved me."

"I have since that day walked around with lightness in my heart, and hope for happiness and well being in His care. We are going to be taken care of, Leeanna. Of this I am sure. The God of our fathers stooped down from His lofty position in Heaven and has spoken to this people with His own words."

Asher's eyes glowed with light.

Allowing these words to soak into my senses, I am astonished at the deep sayings coming from Asher's heart. Suddenly I, too, sensed that all would be well with us. Seeing acceptance on my face, Asher pulled me closer to him and we laughed together in a moment of joy. Nothing could have spoiled this time. We talked a while longer of the great things we had seen with our own eyes and knew it to be of God. Soon, he hurried off to visit Mathias and to invite him to come take bread with us this evening.

My attention is quickly drawn back when the baby began crying from inside the tent. I wanted to linger, talk and rejoice with Asher, but there are other things necessary too.

"God allowed father and I an opportunity to have a glimpse of happiness from atop the mountain today, but the valley where we live calls us back so soon," I whispered to little Andrew while preparing to feed him.

For the rest of the day, I felt like a young woman again. My mind and heart were as light as a feather knowing that God has all of us in His capable hands.

****

The evening meal has been prepared and Mathias finishes the prayer of thanksgiving. Asking our old friend to pray the prayer of thanksgiving indicates a family relationship with us. In the same way, it helps him realize that we accept him into our family as a loved one and is called on in family matters. With Mathias, one need not guess just where he stands concerning family. He has endeared himself to our group with gentleness of character and his offer to help shoulder the work load. If Grandfather was still alive, he would stand no higher in our esteem than Mathias.

"I have something to say to you, Asher and Leeanna," Mathias says, putting his cup down beside his bowl.

Asher and I looked in Mathias's direction, watching his face for any alarming looks. Wiping his hands with the folded napkin, he rises to a sitting position allowing us a brief moment to do the same.

"Speak what is in your heart old friend," Asher replies with a bow of his head and a sweeping motion of his right arm. "You are among family and friends here, feel free to speak at your convenience, my lord."

Mathias bows his head in acceptance of the offer.

"I have thought long and hard on the day's events when the people gathered before the mountain."

Asher and I nodded our heads as Mathias continued.

"As I stood there that day waiting for the Lord to speak, my thoughts turned to years gone past when I was a young man. My beloved wife was as beautiful a woman as any man could want; she had a sweetness within her that could turn away sorrow from any troubled soul. Our home, most of the time, was filled with different ones coming to sit and listen to the wisdom she spoke. She seemed to never grow tired of these souls who adored listening to the stories she told them. They were stories from a time long ago when the Almighty had dealings with the forefathers, Abraham, Isaac, and Jacob. Those times were preserved in the hearts and minds of the people back then and spoken often to their children so the memories would be taught to the following generations. Today, there is almost no knowledge of our forefathers' rich and full past except for a few families who have kept the tradition and passed it on to their children."

Asher and I both adjusted our sitting positions, trying not to look as guilty as we certainly felt.

"I am afraid," Mathias said, "because of this lack of teaching among the people that the words of God spoken to us all that day before the mountain were not received in the deep sense that God desired. Yes indeed, the people heard the words spoken to us, but they were not welcomed in tender hearts. Moses explained the ordinances and meanings of these great sayings, and the people gave their consent that all was understood and agreeable. Our ears heard the teaching of Moses as he read all the words, but our understanding was not and indeed cannot be accomplished in just one hearing. I could attach some of the teaching Moses gave us to what I have learned, listening to the oral traditions. But it is my thought that we all, as a people, must begin to work with each other and spread what we have learned to others. Then the hearts of the people will be turned like a garden in the spring of the year, prepared to receive God's word." Mathias stopped speaking, and drew a deep breath as he waited for our reactions.

My thoughts are in a whirlwind. How many times have I said that I must begin to teach our children? Yet only a few times have I done this. Trying to place myself in the mindset of my children, I wondered what they must be thinking about all that's taken place in the last few days. Asher and I had forgotten to examine their thoughts and answer any questions they might have.

Mathias is certainly right. I am guilty of not teaching our children the ways of the forefathers as they lived and walked under God's care. It is an awakening for me like when little Andrew cries out for his milk and expects to be fed. I also need to feed the children the ways and oral teachings I received from my father and mother.

Asher sits silent a long time before speaking his thoughts. I can feel the pressure from his hand as, unknowingly, he squeezes mine while in deep thought. Asher extends his hands toward Mathias. After Mathias grasps Asher's hands and bow's his head forward in courtesy to his host, only then does Asher speak.

"My friend, what you have shared with my family is fully appreciated and requires me to spend time examining our family's stand on the matters you have described. Even as you spoke, my own heart burned within me attesting to the truthfulness of your words. Because this thing has come upon your heart to say and do, surely it must be ordained from God. I also have seen with my own eyes and have heard the shallowness that comes from the hearts and minds of this great people. Leeanna and I have been blessed. We grew up hearing about the ways of God when He began calling forth a people from the heathen nation of Ur of the Caldees. Our forefathers walked with God through four generations before all of that generation died."

Asher shifted his position before continuing.

"When Jacob went down into Egypt, his twelve sons continued the tradition of worshiping God and passing down the true stories the forefathers passed on to them. But after those twelve passed away, the children born to them began to ignore the old traditions and became absorbed in the many religions throughout that area. From generation down through generation, the traditions became less taught. So the people, after four hundred years, were without knowledge of our great God and unbelief was strong. If our parents' had not persisted in telling us these wonderful truths, then Leeanna and I would be as ignorant and hard-hearted as so many within this camp today. I do not consider myself an authority pertaining to this knowledge, but I am willing to do as you have suggested. I will go to my neighbors rehearsing as much of this history and teachings as God will permit," he stated, raising his right hand and placing it over his heart.

Mathias spoke again. "It is within our power, Asher, to lay the foundation of the faith of our fathers before God's people. We all heard the beautiful words and were witnesses to the glorious sights upon Mt. Horeb. So if we will take this event and begin a campaign as we discussed, the people will eventually experience a hunger for the ways of God while they also see His mighty works with us in our day."

I sat quietly by my husband's side and listened to all the wonderful things he and Mathias talked about. My heart gives assurance that this is a good thing. The future looks brighter as we sit and talk with our friend. What a blessing he surely is!

****

Over the next few days, we notice a change taking place within the attitudes of the camps of Israel. No longer is there an air of quiet communal abode. There is much anger with shouting and a growing distain for Israel's traveling out of the land of Egypt.

Luke and Astoria have been afraid and are staying closer to our tent. They are satisfied playing games with each other rather than with friends. There are riotous voices that suddenly break out, and it is increasingly difficult for the baby to sleep through his naps. Loud arguments mingled with the cries of women and children are becoming more frightening. There are several groups of men who gather and speak harsh words against our leader, Moses. As each day goes by, more men join those groups.

Asher warned me to stay close to our tent for fear of the situation developing around us. Aaron, his two sons', and the seventy elders returned from the mountain to the camp site yesterday. Perhaps they will be able to search out the matter in these growing groups of men and find a way to ease the tension they have caused. Seeking an opportunity to speak to Mathias, after he returned from milking, I ask if he was aware of what the matter could be among the people. His face carried a haggard look as he rested before the fire. I pulled loose a serving of bread, spread it with butter while Astoria poured him a cup of milk and set it before him.

Mathias smiled at her, and placed a hand to his turban in gesture of thank you before directing his attention on me.

"I will not speak in front of the children and not before your husband is here with us. I pray that you will understand my reluctance, dear woman," he said with an anguished expression.

"It is the nature of a man to not speak of worrisome things before a woman, especially since your man is not here to decide if you may hear of such. You are like a daughter to me, and are rest for my eyes every time they look upon you, dear lady. The worry on your face grieves me and causes my heart pain. But since your husband is not here with us at this time, I cannot take this matter from his table. If indeed Asher knows anything about the chaos being generated within the camps of Israel, then it is certainly his decision whether to inform you or to withhold it."

Mathias finished his milk, rose up, and gently patted my shoulder giving me a wink before walking away. Of course, Mathias is right. It is not his place to bring any news to Asher's family unless he was sent by Asher with his permission to do so. I watched as Mathias walked to his tent, his shoulders gently sagging.

"I would love to have known his dear wife," I said to Astoria as he disappeared inside his tent.

"I believe she must have been as smart and as lovely as you are Mama," she replied while cleaning the bowl Mathias had used.

****

"Leeanna," Asher whispered, after the children had gone inside for a nap, "are the children asleep yet?"

Gently walking to the door, I peeked inside and heard their gentle even breathing.

"Yes, I think they have given in to the sleep bug, my dear," I replied, sitting down beside my husband.

Asher appears tired. I asked if he would enjoy a nap also, but he shakes his head and motions toward the other camps in front of us. My mind is bursting to ask if he is aware of what is going on around the camp. But as Mathias said, it is up to Asher whether to tell what he knows or keep it to himself. Asher began talking in hushed tones so the children wouldn't hear.

"There is much fear in the camp, Leeanna. I know you have heard and seen disturbing things for a few days now. There are groups of men spreading lies around the camp, saying Moses has not returned because God has found some disfavor with him and has killed him. They are inciting disorder and speaking of going back to Egypt. I am glad that Aaron and the elders have returned to camp. Maybe now the people will see that since God did not kill them, surely Moses still lives. This is a result of non-belief and faithless hearts just as Mathias talked about. I have tried to speak with these men, but their anger and dullness of hearing has caused my talking and encouragement to come to nothing. Many of the men have resorted to fighting each other and speaking abusive things to their families. With the way it's growing, I want you and the children to stay close by the tent. While I am about my duties, Mathias will stay close to protect you and the children."

"How can this be? Only a few days have come and gone since God spoke to all of the people from the mountain and gave us His commandments! Why should the people listen to such hogwash as these men are spewing? There's a feeling I've had since that day we gathered. It is not explainable, but it is deep within me. I've tried to figure out why it is there! As we talk, it is still there and sadness of heart. Do you think their regression from the faith of the Lord was a sign given to me that very day?" I asked.

"It is sure that what has bothered you has also bothered many others, Leeanna," Asher explains, "Not all of the men have the same thoughts as these few groups. There are many in Israel who do not believe the way those do who stir up the camp against Moses. I am sorry I withheld my own fears about this from you. It is a sad day when the opinions of the few outweigh the hopes of the many. And with all my strength, God willing, we shall stand strong and stand up until the Lord tells us different."

The muscles in his jaw grew tight.

****

Moses has been gone from the camp for such a long time. There is so much chaos and riotous language that my body seems to stay stiff. I am constantly watching and looking about to make sure the children are not harmed. Asher and Mathias go out to tend the herd earlier than ever. Luke is not allowed to run about the camp with the other children. He is upset because Asher will not let him go out with him as before. Asher explained that when he is conducting business with the other men that he must stay in a state of caution against arguing and foul language. Luke has no business hearing all this, though it filters over to our tent most every day.

Where there was once beautiful flute music drifting in the air, there is now music that has a sense of discord and confusion. I am beginning to wonder if Moses will return like so many of the people have been saying. We are in need of fresh water, and neither Asher nor

Mathias is here. Cautioning Astoria to stay near our tent and to listen out for Andrew lest he awaken from his nap, I picked up the water pot, took Luke's hand, and started out.

After a few steps, Luke pulled away from my hand saying he does not want his friends to see him holding his mama's hand like a little child. So allowing this but thinking it is not the best thing to do, I let him have his way. As we walk along, Luke gets several steps ahead of me and sees some of his friends. Calling out to him and holding something in a cloth, they tell him to come over and see.

When Luke runs over and tries to look inside of the cloth, one boy puts out his leg tripping him. When Luke falls to the ground, two boys began kicking him as they laugh and call him names. Rushing forward to stop the mad assault on my son, I reached out to grab one boy just as he tried for another kick at Luke's face. The boys laughed and ran away while Luke is still trying to get up. Suddenly, Luke turns toward me and screams out that I made him look weak in front of his friends. And that he could have wrestled both of them and won too, if it had not been for me interfering.

Immediately, I set down the water pot, took Luke's arm, and, turning him face forward, placed three sound swats across his back end.

"The first swat is for running ahead of me," I informed him, while placing each swat. "The second one is for screaming at me. I am your mother, and you will not ever scream at me, do you hear? The third one is for lying, because you could not wrestle both boys at one time and win. Look at yourself! Your nose is bloody, your eye is swelling, and there are scrapes all over you. Now you really have something to be embarrassed about before your friends. Mama swatted your behind!"

Turning him around to face me, I pointed towards our tent and stomped my foot to let him know just where he was to go. He ran in that direction as fast as he could. I didn't go on for water until he disappeared inside our tent.

Chapter 4

My nerves feel as raw as bread dough as I continue on to get the water. From every direction comes loud, raucous laughter mixed with sordid musical sounds. I quicken my steps so I can get back to the children. Deep inside, I have a sense of foreboding which increases each day.

"Oh please, dear God, please send Moses back to us. He is the only one who can straighten out whatever has become crooked in this place. The people have listened to him in the past, and it is my prayer that they will listen to him now. You have been kind enough to allow your pillar of cloud and pillar of fire to stay visible during all these many days, but there is no voice of authority in the camp as when Moses was here. How long must we wait and endure these tormenting fears? If Moses did indeed die before You on the mountain top, then what are we to do for a leader? What chance do we have if Moses was found with some disfavor in Your sight?" I prayed with a burning heart.

Just as I finished the prayer, a man came stumbling out from a tent and almost collided with me. He began laughing and trying to apologize at the same time. He quickly turns about and takes my arm asking if he may be of service. Responding to his courteous offer, I decline his help as I dislodge my arm from his grip. His face suddenly became distorted with anger and, leering at me, he takes hold of my arm again with a painful grip.

"You should be more careful walking about without your man by your side," he snarls, pushing his face close to mine. "Or could it be that your man was one of the poor souls who lost his life in the battle with Amalek. If that be the case, then please allow me to escort the grieving widow to fetch her water." He tipped his head toward my water pot.

Suddenly someone took hold of my other arm in a firm grasp

and pulled me to one side. I couldn't see who the other person was but I glimpsed a man's robe. Mathias had been near the tent when I sent Luke back, and heard where I'd gone from Luke. The flash of a man's robe was Mathias. He pulled me aside, and with the force of a young man, he shoved his other hand into the stranger's chest sending him sprawling backwards. The stranger quickly picked himself up from the ground and ran away yelling curses over his shoulder.

"Are you harmed in any way, Leeanna?" Mathias asked while continuing to watch the stranger run away.

"No, I am fine, but I thank God that you came by when you did. I came to fetch water, but now I am too shaken to continue on." I wondered if my legs had the strength to even carry me.

Reaching out for my water pot, Mathias said that he would walk me back to my tent and then go fetch water once I was safely home.

When we arrived, Luke was wiping his face with a damp cloth, and Astoria was fussing over him trying to help. The excited voices outside our tent had awakened Andrew, and he was crying. Pressing my hands against my ears, I sat down sobbing, rocking back and forth. Mathias went inside, picked up Andrew, and laid him across his broad chest as he patted the baby's back. Luke and Astoria both watched me crying with their eyes as big as saucers. Luke came over to me, placed his head in my lap, and told me he was sorry for being disrespectful. Mathias patted Luke on the shoulder as he walked past us to retrieve a diaper from the basket for the baby. I am so grateful for his help, and now I know to listen to him and Asher when they warn us for our own safety.

Asher hurried into the tent to see about me after hearing what happened. Mathias insisted that I lie down for a rest and leave the children in his care.

"I am so thankful you are not harmed," Asher said after having had a chance to question me. "Why would you go away from the safety of our tent and risk your safety and that of the children, too? I thought I made myself clear to you about the conditions around this camp, Leeanna. Each day that passes gets more dangerous than the last since Moses has not returned. We are fortunate that Mathias was able to handle the stranger who tried to molest you. But what would have become of you had he not been so able or close to where you were? Luke is only a child, and would not have been able to help you."

"Asher," I pleaded, "please forgive me for not obeying your warning. It was a foolish mistake. I was not as aware of the debased conditions about camp as you and Mathias. The children and I have been close by our tent for weeks, and we did need fresh water. So without much thought, I decided to fetch the water myself as I have done for a long time. I would never have thought that something as horrible as what could have happened to me today would have ever been done by an Israelite. What kind of spirit is at work in these people, and what kind of people are we traveling with that we must stay hidden behind the walls of our tent to stay safe?"

Once again the tears began streaming down my face as the thought of what almost happened is refreshed in my mind. Asher reached for my hands and pulled them away from my face. Searching my face, he pulled me close to his chest and smoothed my hair down the length of my back. He began kissing my forehead and moved on to my neck as he held me close to him. I needed the comfort of his lips on mine and finally they meet. Murmuring words of love and sweetness in my ear, he gently laid me back on the mat again with his arms still enclosing me.

"You are safe now, sweet Leeanna," he whispers, "safe in my arms and in the place where you belong, with me and the children who love you. Sleep now, sweet pet, and I will help Mathias with the children," He arose and withdrew from the room.

I can hear the men talking in hushed tones outside our tent. Asher and Mathias are finishing the day's chores, and I feel guilty for not being on my feet to help them. Trying to rise up from the mat, a wave of dizziness comes over me, so I decide to stay lying down for a while longer.

Suddenly the sound of a trumpet fills the air, and I jumped with fright. What does this sound mean and from whom has the command to blow the trumpet come? Managing to sit up again, I wait a bit before rising to my feet. Walking to the tent door, I looked out and saw Asher walking away from our tent in a hurry. Mathias is sitting with the baby in his arms, and he looks around at me as I walk out the door. Seeing the look on my face, he simply shakes his head and shrugs his shoulders, telling me he is not aware of the meaning of the trumpet sound. My knees feel weak beneath me, as I stare out across the camp, watching Asher disappear around the side of a tent. Pointing toward a stool, Mathias urges me to sit down and asked if I felt well enough to hold Andrew while he continued scraping the goat hide. I assured him that I was fine as long as I remained sitting down. He laid the baby in my arms, and waited to see if I was able to handle the child.

Luke and Astoria were playing a game called Marbles. It is played with several small stones heaped together and a slightly larger round stone is used for thumping toward the other pile of stones. They are playing together so well and are not arguing, which is a big relief in itself.

I watched as Mathias stretched the goat hide securely to the wooden stand with the fur side down so he could scrape away the thin layer of fat and flesh on the reverse side. Waiting and wondering about my husband's safety causes more stress. I cannot seem to clear my mind from the earlier events of the day. Pulling my head covering across my chest, I reached into the bodice of my robe and loose one breast to feed the baby. After a while, Andrew begins to squirm and fuss, moving his mouth away. I immediately shifted him to the other side to receive suck. Soon the baby begins to squirm and cry loudly against my chest, moving his head side to side as if searching for more milk. What is wrong with this child I ask myself? I tried again to give him suck from my breast. He acts like he is hungry, but why isn't he drinking? Rising up from the stool and carrying the baby into the tent, I try to give him suck several more times, but the same pattern repeats again.

"Oh God, what is wrong with this child?" I said aloud as frustration and more worry flooded my heart.

I then tried to squeeze milk from my breast so I can dip the corner of a cloth into the milk and put it into Andrew's mouth. Fear envelops me as I try to empty milk from one breast into a small bowl, but no milk will come out. Trying the other one brings the same result.

"There is nothing wrong with the baby, but there is something wrong with me," I whispered. "Mathias, I have to go across the way to speak to Jillian on a private matter. I am taking Andrew so you can continue your work on the hide and not be bothered with the baby. Please would you be so kind to keep an eye on the other children? If Asher should return before I come back, tell him where we have gone."

Without giving Mathias an opportunity to reply, I quickly start the short walk to Jillian's tent. Luke and Astoria ran to me as I crossed the small space between my tent and Jillian's.

"Mama, where are you and the baby going? Can we come along with you?" they began to chime in pleading voices.

Without slowing my pace, I commanded them to go back to the tent and stay where Mathias can watch over them, and no, they may not come along this time. I sense Mathias's eyes watching every step I take as my mission to Jillian's intensifies. I have no time to explain my rush out the door to anyone, and I pray that Jillian will be there when we arrive.

I tried to be polite, but the urgency in my voice belies my feeble attempt.

"Jillian, are you in there?"

Jillian rushes out of the tent door with a concerned look on her face.

"Leeanna!" she asked, "Is there something wrong? You sound terrified! But with all that's happening around camp, who is not terrified?"

"Are you alone inside your dwelling at this time Jillian? There is a matter of utmost importance which I must speak with you about," I asked in a hushed tone.

"Yes, my dear. Unfortunately my husband is out somewhere trying to soothe the nerves of a lot of people. So many people are in a state of panic and do not know what is to become of us since Moses has not returned to be our leader."

But seeing the sheer terror on my face, Jillian put her arm around my shoulder and walked me inside where we can be assured of privacy.

"I have no milk in my breasts for the baby," I blurted out as we entered the dwelling. "I don't know why my breasts have become empty. When I tried to feed Andrew, no milk came. Please tell me. What do you think is wrong with me? How can such as this happen? He is but a few weeks born, and this did not befall me with the other two children when they were babies."

Jillian's look of concern increased as she studied on what I told her. Twisting her body toward me so she could watch my face, she looked directly in my eyes as she spoke.

"Leeanna, is everything good between you and Asher? Please answer my questions without being embarrassed dear. I must ask about things which you may not wish to answer, but in order to find out the cause of this problem, you must be honest with me. Tell me all the truth and withhold nothing."

"Yes, oh yes, Jillian," I assured her, "our relationship is very good. Why would you think that could cause such a problem as this?"

Jillian shook her head and replied, "Dear one, if you have experienced any marital problems, this can bring stress in your body. Stress could cause certain natural functions in your body to not work correctly. Now, what has happened over the last day, which might bring stress or severe worry on you?" She reached to take Andrew into her arms. "Leeanna, for the love of our blessed God, tell me what has happened to you!"

Seeing the alarm which came upon my face, she reached out and placed her hand on my cheek. Dropping my head down toward my lap, the tears ran down my face. After a while, I was finally able to tell Jillian about what happened when I went to fetch water today. Jillian sat calmly and nodded her head as I continued rehearsing the ordeal to her.

She did not interrupt at any time, allowing all the time I needed to complete the details. I started with Luke's fight, then the encounter with the stranger, and after arriving back to my tent escorted by Mathias, the baby was crying, and Astoria was fussing over Luke's face. Luke was sullen and angry at me for swatting him, and it all became too much to handle. Mathias took over the situation and ordered me to go inside and lie down for a spell. But the horrible thoughts of what could have happened kept assaulting my mind. After Asher had come in to check on me, I tried to get up to help the men with the chores, but a wave of dizziness overwhelmed me, so I laid back down.

"It was after Asher left to find out the reason for the trumpet being blown that I went to feed Andrew and realized my milk had dried up!"

I finished explaining to Jillian, and looked desperately into her eyes for any answer she might have.

"Leeanna, your body and mind have been through a lot of briars today, and your body has simply decided to shut down for a spell and rest. God, in His great wisdom, put within us a valve, so to speak, which will turn off when there is too much pressure. The release of pressure can at times create total havoc in one's self or to others. God has said that He will not place anymore on us than we can bear, and today you had your basket full. So to save you from total breakdown, your body simply reacted to danger and decided simply to release no more than it needs to keep you intact. Your milk will return to your breasts, but only after your body has rested for a while and senses safety. I will contact a wet nurse to feed Andrew until you are able to resume feeding him from your own breasts. I will make all the arrangements with your approval, of course, and come to fetch you when we are ready. Since the baby has not eaten for several hours, it is best we get started on this quickly." Jillian assured me.

****

Chapter 5

" **A**sher, what you are telling us has nothing to do with today!" Amadeus squawked. "All you have said is likely true and very interesting, but these stories are ancient and have no bearing on our plight today."

"No, you are wrong brother! Please, fellow Israelites, I beg of you, do not listen with only your ears, but listen also with your hearts. Our forefathers walked with God for many generations. This was passed down to us and will help us to understand God's plan for our lives as individuals and as a nation, a nation raised up and called out by the mighty workings of God. Why would God have rescued this great company of Israelites from the hardships of Egypt if He had no great plan and future to unfold before us? We are in the early stages of learning how to become a nation of people being led by the Lord God Almighty. He is well able to bring us to the place which He promised our fathers. If indeed this Moses was found to have some disfavor in God's sight, then God is able to raise up another leader from these stones in like manner of Moses to lead this great congregation. Let not your hearts fear. Neither be fools in discerning what spirit is at work in some of this congregation. Do not turn your minds from following the commands of the Lord. He gave us these commands with His own voice, and they will bring us through these uncertain times. Be of one voice again, O men of Israel, as we were of one voice before Mt. Horeb that faithful day. We must come together and take heed of what can be learned and what is still visible above the top of this mountain. This is a sign of God's presence and faithfulness for all to see. Has God withheld the manna each morning from us, or has He withdrawn the quail in the evening for our meat? The voice of Moses at this time is silent, but the promises of God are still here with us in all these things of which I have spoken. If God had deserted His people, then why would He not just take away our sustenance and our water and allow us to die here in this wilderness? No brothers! God has not abandoned His people, Israel, neither now nor ever. Can you understand this?" Asher shouted trying to raise his voice above those arguing against him.

Shoving Asher aside, Amadeus takes the lead in the conversation, "What you are saying brings no comfort and leaves this congregation to the whims of the gods to toy with us and lead us into destruction. Men of Israel! Listen to my voice, and you will see the way in which we must go. We are not so far from Egypt that we cannot return again and perhaps find favor with Pharaoh. The route back has springs of water still; we saw them with our own eyes, did we not? There are enough cattle producing a fresh supply of milk and meat to sustain us for the journey. Where is this great leader Moses which brought us to this place of barren wasteland? Is he not dead and his body wasting in decay up in that mountain?" he shouts as he points his stubby finger in the direction of the mountain. "We will make a god to go before us and protect us, O Israel!" he declares while others join their voices in shouts of agreement.

Waving his arms in the air, Asher tries for room to speak again. This kind of talk being spewed out to the growing group is poison and sheer disobedience. The volume of their voices slowly grows quiet and allows him a place to speak.

In Israel, men are not accustomed to doing some deed without complete discussion from all interested parties. Not all who stand here saying such bold things are of Israel but are stragglers who came out with Israel when redemption came from Egypt. If these men were men of wisdom and were elders in Israel, their speeches would be honored, in turn, as each wished to speak. It is the way of men to honor the elders and pay heed to their words, but even that portion of hospitality is quickly eroding. No one is obliged to follow advice when a matter is presented before them, but to listen with a heart of discernment, has great wisdom, even to the fool.

Asher begins to speak with as much veracity as he could muster, praying in his heart for wisdom to dispel Amadeus' derision.

"When father Abraham came out from Ur, he did not know where he was to go, brethren. He knew he had a promise from God, a promise which was refreshed to him over and over again. This same God, which led Abraham throughout the rest of his days, is the God who spoke to all Israel only a few weeks ago. Father Abraham journeyed throughout a vast land, living in tents, waiting, and looking for the promise of God to be fulfilled. Yet as he journeyed, he was always shown the way to go and was miraculously provided for by his mighty

Benefactor. That great promise was also handed down throughout the generations of Abraham's children, Isaac and Jacob. We are the descendants of the seed of Jacob. Starting with our deliverance from Egyptian captivity by the powerful arm of Almighty God up to where we are now, you must reason in your minds how God is setting the stage for the total fulfillment of that promise in us and for us. A land, brethren, a land of our own, a land we can settle on, a land where we will never be strangers again. A land of abundance and plenty, a land teaming with possibilities, a land reserved for us by God, a land where our children may grow up and be free of bondage. A land so vast there is room for our entire nation to live in peace and security, a land touched by God!"

After saying this, Asher begins to praise God and worship Him, hoping others would join him in this devotion.

"If God intends to honor this mighty promise as you say, then where is our leader and where is this wonderful land? Is it behind that hill or maybe beyond that mountain? Perhaps it is a dream that faded a long time ago," shouted a taunting voice. "You do not think, do you, that we are going to stay the rest of our days out here in this wilderness with nothing to eat but this manna? Where are the grassy plains, the trees full of fruit, the garlic, leeks, onions, and fish which we had in abundance in Egypt? Why do you fight against us using all these words, and painting beautiful pictures in our minds, when all we can see before us is this desert and hardship?"

Asher responded saying, "You cannot see what is before you because you have talked yourselves into blindness. Hope is not hope when it can be looked on. Then it is hope no more. It has become a reality. We have this blessed hope before our faces, and what God is doing for us now will become a reality when the promise has been brought to pass. If we are hasty with this thing Amadeus proposes, then we will be guilty of turning our backs on God and throwing Gods promise back in His face. Do you indeed miss the days of slavery so much that you can barely wait to be yoked to that plow again? Were you and your families so in love with your lives in Egypt that you would risk having them destroyed at the hands of Pharaoh? What about your children? They have nothing to look forward to, but a lifetime of crooked backs carrying bricks to increase Pharaoh's mansions of grandeur. Was the ease of leisure why we all cried out to God for salvation, or was it the everyday hard toil of our families under the rod of an unjust dictator who hated and abused us? Answer me if you can! When there was no water along our journey these last months, who did you cry out to? Was it Pharaoh? Maybe you called out to Baal. Perhaps it was one of the many idols which are stone carvings that have no ears or eyes? No! I will tell you Who you called out to! We all cried out to God and He heard us and gave us the water we thirsted for. Where is your faith brethren?"

"Words, words, words! So many ungrounded words," says a new arrival to the group. "All these eloquent words, and no one to clap their hands for your delivery of these words," he snarled. "You are the one who is blind my friend, and you have nothing of value to say. We have stood and listened to this fellow blow his horn for too long. Let us come together and make definite arrangements for our return back to where we will be welcomed, the land of our birth, back to Egypt!" The crowd began following his oratory with shouts of "Back to Egypt, O Israel!"

Asher is almost knocked to the ground as the people surge past him with shouting and fists waving in the air. The mob of men moved towards Aaron's encampment. One man has a ram's horn which he continuously blows. More people came running toward the sound of the horn, and soon the dust stirred up by the crowd's feet distorts Asher's vision. He watches as they make their way toward the center of the camps with children running close at the heels of the mob. Falling to his knees, Asher spreads forth his hands and cries out to God for mercy toward this stiff-necked and hard-hearted people.

****

Aaron heard the sound of the horn blowing and becomes nervous as the sound nears his dwelling.

"My brother, Moses, should be here and take control of this crowd," he thinks to himself. Hearing his own name being called out brings his knees to a state of weakness. "Why must I have the worry of all these people?" He whispered and then stepped out to meet them face to face.

****

"Lord, I tried to tell them," Asher prayed aloud, "but they will not listen to me."

Asher felt a hand press against his shoulder and a voice says, "Neither did they listen to us."

Opening his eyes and looking toward the sound of the voice, Asher is surprised to see a large group of men behind him, and they all nod their heads in agreement. Rising to his feet, Asher recognizes many of the elders of Israel among them. Wiping his tear-soaked eyes, Asher's heart began to settle down. The elder of the Asher clan placed his hand on top of Asher's head and the other hand on his shoulder.

"As each day passed into the next since the day Moses disappeared into the thick cloud upon the top of Mt. Horeb, the crowds have increased in their disbelief. I have watched many good and wise men of Israel giving heed to their fears and become as mad dogs prowling about the camps," he informs Asher. "They have become as ravaging lions looking for whom they could devour with their sordid speeches. Many of the weaker, less experienced people gave them attention, and now their smoldering speeches have become a raging fire, threatening to devour us all. We do not yet know the damage these firebrands have done, but, as our breaths are still within our bodies, we will try to reach into that fire and snatch some back from total destruction. God be praised that you, my son, have a heart of wisdom and love for the ways of our forefathers. Join your efforts with ours as we make a stand against this evil plan they are making." The others voiced their agreement to this request.

"What more can we do or say that will soften their resistant hearts?" Asher asked as the old man looked into his eyes. "Do they not have eyes in their heads to see God's provision for all Israel? Do they not have ears that heard God's mighty voice when He spoke to us? And concerning all the ordinances Moses read to us that came from the very mouth of God, how can they dismiss it as if it were a dream?"

"The people have depended on a man to lead them," replied the elder, "and have not depended on God. Some requested of Moses to let God speak to him and not to us because they were afraid to hear His voice. God has shaken their dependency on man with the long absence of Moses. Our God desires all men to depend directly on Him for His guidance and for our daily bread. Man cannot live by bread alone but by every word which comes from God. If a wise teacher of men becomes a fool, then he will cause himself and his followers to fall in a ditch. Our God is all wise, and there is no darkness in His turning. There is no perverted bias toward anyone, no lack of understanding, and no insufficiency of supply. He is no promise breaker and is powerful enough to do so much more than we can think or ask of Him. If God is for us, and He surely is, then who can stand before Him and bring accusation against Him?"

As the old man talked, tears began to slide down Asher's cheeks. Hearing such a glorious testimony of God's grace has renewed his heart, and he is overwhelmed with a feeling of warmth in his very being. A strange yet powerful feeling took control of his senses as he fed on every word the old man said. He wanted to stay in this feeling of warmth and love for a while longer and wondered if he would ever be able to display such beautiful truths to others who needed to hear them.

As if reading Asher's mind, the elder told him, "As you continue to pay close attention to the words of God and study them in your heart and mind, they will become food for your soul. And they will produce seeds of instruction which you will be able to scatter abroad to many people who have the opportunity to cross your path in life. God is well able to teach you, and He desires each person to learn. He is able to bring all manner of hearts before you to plant those seeds in. One will do the plowing, one will do the planting, and one will do the watering. But it is God himself Who will give the increase." Elder Jarrod concluded.

Asher hoped he would be able to retain all this information so he could repeat it to Leeanna and Mathias. Even as he thought this, he became aware that he must also teach these things to his children. Here I am, he thought, enjoying all these wonderful things I have heard and have almost forgotten to include my children. This is one of the main reasons why Israel had very little knowledge of God for over four hundred years. Not many had heard the teachings from their fathers.

"Come tonight after the evening meal," the Elder said, "and join our group as we listen and enjoy what each one shares on the ways of God. God is a rewarder, and He will reward those who hunger and thirst after righteousness, my son. Of this, you can be sure."

Turning his head toward where the crowd had gone earlier, he began walking in that direction. The rest of the group followed. As each man passed Asher, he would put out his hand and brush Asher's shoulder saying "my brother" as he passed by.

Asher stood in the same place for a long time, remembering all that had taken place. Soon, he became aware that a few children had gathered around him and were giggling. He made a great gesture for them.

He placed his arm across his waist and gave a deep bow saying, "And now children of Israel, I must leave your company and retreat to my own tent for lunch. The next time we meet, I will perform one of my best songs for your enjoyment, if that pleases you. If not, perhaps you can watch me stand on my head in the hot sand until my ears smoke!"

He finished with a flip of his head shawl and galloped away mimicking a horse as the children's laughter echoed behind him.

****

Mathias was still scraping the goat hide when I returned to the tent.

"I'm sorry I rushed out from here without leaving an explanation." I said, noticing the hurt look on his face.

"I was in a panic before and needed to speak to Jillian. I hope you are not too upset with me." Reaching down and lifting his face up so I could see his eyes I said, "Your face gives you away. Dear friend, there are some things that a woman needs to talk over with another woman, and I pray you understand."

Watching his face, it becomes clear that the edge of hurt is leaving his expression. Mathias took a deep breath and laid aside the flint rock he was using to scrape the hide.

"If something more had befallen you, Leeanna, such as happened this morning, I do not think Asher would forgive me for not protecting you. Nor could I forgive myself. Whatever the reason was for your hurried departure earlier is, of course, your business. But please try to take enough time before you rush away so I can escort you and try to keep harm from you!" he replied, spreading his palms out above the hide and tilting his head to one side.

The twinkle in his eyes let me know he had accepted my explanation. To see his concern, put a warm feeling in my heart. How fortunate to be blessed with such a dear elder of Israel. He is a friend, and a mentor who cares for us and is willing to place our safety before his.

As I started into the tent, Astoria and Luke were just waking from their naps and came out rubbing the sleep from their eyes.

"You were gone for a long time, Mama. We were wondering when you would be back." Luke says, while wrapping his arms around my legs.

"It wasn't that long, Luke," Astoria shot back at him. "You make it sound like she was gone for all day!"

"Did not!" he answers.

"Did too!" Astoria countered back.

"Did not," Luke says again.

"Did too," Astoria yells.

"Are you two going to tug that same rope back and forth all day?" Mathias asked. "If you have finished your tug of war, come and help me prepare lunch. You can tug back and forth with this grinding stone over the manna for our bread!"

The children quickly forgot their disagreement and hurried to obey Mathias's command.

Having the children occupied gave me a chance to thank God properly for the wet nurse Jillian located for Andrew. Being upset over my breasts not producing milk, Jillian decided it was best I wait in her tent while she went to fetch Gretchen so Andrew could be fed. Arrangements were made with Gretchen to come to my tent in a few hours for the next feeding. Laying the baby on my mat and gently covering him, I pressed my heart before the Lord in prayer for all His glorious blessings.

The squeals of the children calling out to their father brought me back to myself and aware of where I was. What a wonderful time spent with God! I felt as though my body was left behind and my heart soared like an eagle. It was as if I was lifted far above every problem and stared into a beautiful glass sea while sitting beneath a tree of fragrant blossoms. My body felt limp, and there was a warm glow all around me as I lay beside Andrew giving thanks to God for the wonderful experience He gave me. A sweet Voice full of kindness told me that the wet nurse would not be needed any longer, that I would be able to feed my child from my own breasts. Somehow I just knew that Voice was the Voice of God, and, as I drifted off to sleep, I felt safe and comforted again.

****

Asher was sitting outside when I emerged from the tent after my nap.

"Mathias has gone over to his tent for a short nap." Asher said when he saw me looking toward the place Mathias had been working. "This gives me a chance to spend some time with you and tell you all about the day's happenings." He rose up and reached for the bowl of food Mathias had saved for me.

He removed the cloth covering the bowl and offered it to me. Shaking my head, I told him I was not hungry. He put the bowl back in its place and returned to his seat.

I finished pouring a cup of milk and then joined him. These days, it is very rare to have time alone with my husband with all that's taken place over the last few weeks. There is so much to talk about, but where to begin was my thought. I needed to tell Asher about not having breast milk to feed little Andrew. But drawing faith from my prayer to God earlier, I felt the topic would be an unnecessary worry and burden on his mind. And God knows that Asher has a plate full of worries enough for now.

Deciding to be still until another time, I sipped from the cup of milk, gave Asher a smile, and asked him about his morning. As I listened to Asher relaying all the events, I could see a change had invaded his demeanor. No longer did his face have a look of exhaustion and tightness. His speech was full of energy and confidence as if hope had again taken root in his heart. Within me was a feeling of confirmation as I listened closely to him. He told me about the crowd rebuffing his attempts to reason with them, but even this news failed to assuage my confidence. There is surely something happening in our hearts and attitudes. It seems that the trials and troubles we have experienced thus far in our journey have strengthened us and developed our faith, too. We know we are on a journey to the promise land even through this wilderness of life. It is better to know we are headed on God's chosen road of life while He guides every step we take, and the end to come will be glorious.

"We are invited to come and gather with others and be involved in the teachings. If only you could have been there, Leeanna. My heart burned within me as he spoke all those eloquent truths. You would have heard what was said and saw with your own eyes that there are others who stand against this degenerate proposal of the renegades. God has not left us without a witness and, though many have little knowledge of God in this camp of Israel, they are willing to be faithful and listen. The elder holds these group talks every evening after the meal. He is putting his hand to the plow, Leeanna, and others are casting this seed abroad into the hearts of the unlearned." Asher said, while I stared in fascination.

"If there were someway I could go with you and listen, it would be such a blessing," I replied. Wondering if Mathias could watch the children, "Maybe we could impose for a short time each evening on Mathias to watch the children. Of course, I would take Andrew along."

"But that is the kind of thinking we need to get away from!" Asher countered so quickly that it startled me.

"What do you mean by saying that, Asher?" I said letting the volume of my voice rise. "Is it alright for the men to attend and learn all this great truth about God, sharing with each other the blessing of knowledge, but it is forbidden to the women? I saw the presence of God with my female eyes and so did all the other women. I heard His beautiful voice with my female ears and so did all the other women. Do you men think that God only speaks to men, and the women have no business in such holy things? If that be the case, then I advise you against such pure folly! Not often do men take the time with their own children and teach them the ways of God. So do tell, how can a woman expect to learn what she needs to know except through God? As a woman lays on her bed at night, after all the household is sound asleep, her day will not end before she cries out to God for every member of her house and all the trials of each one's day. In the still quietness of the night, she waits for that Voice which she has come to call God, the Voice which comforts and quiets her soul, the Voice which brings strength to face another day, the Voice which commands her mind, "Peace! Be still." She will not rest until she hears that Voice and the assurance that God is in control."

Asher was staring at me with eyes wide open when I finished. He had never heard this confession from me and was looking at me as if he were seeing me for the first time. I started to rise up from the stool to go inside the tent and allow some time for my temper to quiet down. But reaching out, Asher grasped my hand and stopped my intention.

"I am not ready for this Asher!" I said, trying to release his hand from mine. "There has been too much happened today, and my body is weak from the shock of it all." I thought I was going to hear a long lecture on how a woman has no right meddling in men's affairs.

"Leeanna," Asher began, "I had no intention of leaving you, the children, nor Mathias out of the meeting. When I said that was the kind of thinking we needed to get away from, I meant that the men have, in most cases, left the families out when meetings took place. Now it's clear to me that was a big mistake, especially when learning about God. Our families must share together in the wonderful truths discussed so that no one is left out. For this very reason, most of Israel, have very little knowledge of the old ways. Word of mouth, most times, got no further down to the family after it passed the ears of the hearer. I want my family to have all the knowledge we can gather about the old ways which instructs us about God. As far as teaching our children, I have been no better with it than my fellow Israelites." He said. Then I began to relax from the tension that stiffened my body.

"How many are there who still believe as we do, Asher? Are there a handful, twenty, fifty? How many of Israel has decided not to bend the knee to strange gods? I haven't had an opportunity to go out amongst them for weeks, and, judging by the hideous sounds that float throughout the camps, I was afraid there were only a few. Where are they located from where we are? How many will stand with us as we make our way toward the meeting? Will it be safe for the children? Will it be safe for even the adults? Just what are the conditions of the people throughout Israel, Asher?"

"Please settle down, Leeanna. I know you haven't been allowed to walk and visit about the camps as you once did. It is for your own safety and the safety of the children that I forbade you to go out. Most of the people have shown disappointment in one way or another since Moses has not returned, and some have been more outspoken than others. There is a feeling of hopelessness that sweeps its ugly head among the people, and many have fallen prey to its lies but not all have been snared by it. The group I told you about has been hard at work trying to dispute the lies and have been able to save a few from this despair. The work is abundant, and the workers are few. The people are looking for a man to lead them and have not trusted their hearts to the leadership of God. They are not as learned as others in the things of God. But when the truth is made plain to them, and the veil has been taken away from their eyes, they are able to see the hope again!"

"I wonder where and when all this will end, Asher? It is a sobering thought for one to feel he is on the threshold of glory at one time and soon finds his own heart can turn around and plunge from that high peak onto a pile of rocks below." I murmured, shaking my head in astonishment as tears filled my eyes.

****

Chapter 6

"Eat it, just eat it!" Luke taunts Astoria with a firm voice. "You said you wanted to grow taller and be able to run and climb like the boys, did you not? Well, this is what these berries will help you do! You don't have to chew them. Just put them in your mouth and swallow them quickly so you won't make a bad face from the taste."

Astoria slowly examines the tiny berries and vigorously rubs away the dust clinging to them. After taking a deep breath, she shoves them into her mouth and swallows as quickly as she can.

"There," she said, "I have done it."

She giggles as she allows a large burp to escape her mouth and looks at Luke for his approval of her bravery. His eyes are large and full of surprise. He is amazed she really did eat the berries he picked. He wondered what if she doesn't grow big and tall and his friends find out that he lied to his sister. Oh well, maybe they will think he is real smart and brave for this, and it will help him look tougher in their eyes.

"Wonder how tall I will get and how high I can climb now?" Astoria thinks aloud.

"Why, you have just swallowed them, silly girl! You have to give them a few days to start working on growing your muscles and bones bigger and stronger. Could take as long as six or four days before you can really tell how it's working."

"Well, I have done it. So now all that's left is to wait and see what happens," Astoria said, assuring him the deed had been done.

Then, she stood up from her kneeling position. Brushing the sand from her knees, Astoria walked from behind the tent and saw her parents quietly talking in front. Running back around the tent again, she warns Luke that it is best that Mama and Papa not know about the berries. Luke looks up, gives a nod of agreement, and she slowly walks back to the front. Astoria walked over to the small table and poured a cup of milk while listening to our conversation. Noticing her arrival, Asher called out to her and announced the family's plans for after dinner.

Turning to me, she asked, "Mama, where did you go this morning, and why was Mathias looking so worried when you went out?"

Asher quickly turned his head toward me with a questioning look on his face.

"What is Astoria talking about Leeanna? Were you out and about the camps again today after I left?" He asked me. "Wasn't this morning enough for you and must you continue to disobey my warnings concerning your safety when I am gone?"

Astoria was watching me closely to hear my response, so I had to explain everything. I had thought not to worry Asher with my problem today, but thanks to my child, I was forced to explain what had taken place. After briefly answering Astoria's question, I sent her to play and then turned my attention to Asher.

His face by this time had become red and distorted and the look of fire was in his eyes. Why, oh why, I thought, do times of pleasantry have to roll down the hill of anger and wind up destroyed? It is for sure that when one has rejoiced with God on the mountain of glory as I had earlier today, that when you come back down you find you must still live this earthly life in the valley. Asher had gotten up from his stool and was standing before me with his hands propped on his sides. As quickly and as thoroughly as I could, I began the whole story ending with the Voice assuring me that no wet nurse would be needed. I would feed my own son from my own breasts. Asher dropped down again onto the stool with a look of disbelief on his face.

"You thought it was not necessary to tell me about this, did you?" he said, through tight thin lips. "I am out trying to persuade others to listen to reason while I think my wife is safe at home. I fully understand why you had to go to Jillian's but fail to understand why you chose not to tell me about this problem. Andrew's care is my concern just as your care is my concern. If I have failed to give enough time to you so we can share such matters together, then I will stay here and go out no more. Please Leeanna. Do not feel that you must shelter me from any of your life. We agreed to live our lives together. You and the children are my life, and when anything comes along concerning you, tell me about it, please! Thank you for trying to spare me, but I have the need and the right to know." he said, looking directly into my eyes.

"I understand Asher, but with all that has taken place in these last days I did not want to put anything more on you. It was foolish of me to withhold such a thing as important as this, and it will not happen again. Will you please forgive me? And will you allow that beautiful smile to come back again and be rid of those tight lips?" I said, watching him blush.

"Now," he said with a warm smile, "what about tonight? Is it a "family date" and shall I pick you up in a golden, horse-drawn carriage, my lovely wife?"

"No, my lord, a simple goat and cart would please this brood. A carriage would only cause our fine clothes to pale in the gleam of all that gold." We laughed at the thought of it all.

Mathias rounded the corner of our tent just in time to hear me answer Asher's request.

"That is some pretty fancy talk about the gleam of gold dulling your fine clothes, missy," he said, as he bowed indicating his request to join us.

Asher, with his face blushing again, indicates to Mathias his welcome with a finger brushing the side of his turban. We broke out again into peals of laughter as Mathias settled himself on a stool.

"To hear the sound of delicious laughter again makes my old heart glad," Mathias began, looking at Asher and then at me. "Tell me, if I may intrude on your joy, what has brought about this delightful mood?" Mathias's eyes twinkle as he waits for our laughter to subside.

Asher began to explain about the meeting we were invited to attend, and that he and I had been playing rolls to entertain each other at the moment of his arrival.

Upon hearing this news, Mathias's face became serious. He listened intently, nodding his head upon the completion of each point Asher made. Excitement caused his voice to crack.

"This is exactly what we talked about a few days before. This has great potential, and it makes me happy to hear that such a movement is underway for our people. First we must attend and listen to the brethren for ourselves. If what they teach agrees with God's word, then we have a sure destiny every evening, Asher."

While the men continued their talk, I decided to go inside and check on the baby. I had heard some movement earlier as Asher and I talked but had not gone inside to see if he was awake.

My screams brought both men quickly through the tent opening. I was desperately looking all around the room for my baby. His little blanket was there on the mat, but the baby was not under the blanket. Grasping his blanket and holding it against my chest, I began to push everything in my path out of the way as I searched for him. I could faintly hear Asher's voice saying something, but the roar in my ears kept me from understanding his words. I remember that he grabbed my shoulders and was shaking me just before everything in my sight suddenly went black. I do not know how much time passed before I woke up and slowly began to remember what had happened.

Jillian was standing over me with a damp cloth in her hand which she mopped across my face. Her eyes were red as if she had been crying, and her face was damp. Everything came rushing back to me when I turned my head to where the baby normally lay and saw that he was not there. Jillian was saying something, but I was already getting up and frantically calling out my baby's name. Rushing out the tent door, I almost collided with Asher coming inside.

"Where is my baby?" I screamed at him as if he was the one responsible for Andrew's disappearance.

"Leeanna!" Asher said with tears forming in his eyes and a look of torment on his face.

"Get out of my way; I have to find my child. Why do you stand here? Why are you not looking for our son?" I screamed out and tried to push past him.

"Stop this," Asher replied with a strong voice, "Andrew is safe. Mathias has him tucked in his arms. Look for yourself! The baby is not missing. He is here with us Leeanna!"

He grasped my chin and forced my face toward where Mathias was sitting, holding Andrew. The other two children by his side were watching the scene before them in great earnest.

"Give me my child!" I screamed at Mathias and rushed toward him, my arms outstretched. "Why did you take him from me? Why would you do such a terrible thing as this?"

Mathias began shaking his head and pulled the baby closer to his chest while watching me. Asher pulled on the back of my shoulders and turned me around to face him as I struggled to get away so I could take my baby.

"Let me go, Asher! Don't you care that he stole our child from the safety of our tent?" I screamed, gasping for breath.

"Leeanna! Mathias did not steal our son from us. You have had a bad dream." Asher shouted while struggling to keep me still. "When you went into the tent earlier to check on Andrew, you fainted just as you walked in the tent. Mathias and I managed to pick you up and laid you on your mat. He picked up the baby so I could tend to you. I fetched Jillian to come and help me take care of you. You have been babbling about the baby being gone, and we were afraid you were sick with fever. It was all a horrible dream, dear one, just a horrible dream."

It took a while for his words to soak into my senses. My hands and knees were shaking, and my chest heaving. Taking in gulps of air to cool the fire in my throat from all the screaming, I sank down, with Asher's help onto a stool. Lifting my weary eyes to Mathias, I began to beg his forgiveness for my accusations against him. His eyes had a sign of tears as he put out a hand toward me, motioning for me to stop, that my apology was not necessary.

"I will lay the child in your arms as soon as we know you are calm enough to hold him." Mathias said in a gentle and tender voice. "I would not let you have him before because, in your condition, you were not able to hold him, dear woman."

The other two children ran to me and hugged my shoulders as I began crying.

Jillian stood in the tent door watching the scene; after I had calmed down she gently helped me into the tent.

"She will be fine now," she assured those watching, "I will help her inside and return for the baby as soon as she is settled." We made our way through the door.

Jillian left the room to take Andrew from Mathias's arms and came back right away. As she placed the baby in my arms, I pulled him as close to my heart as I could without smothering him.

"God be praised that you, little one, are safe after all," I whispered.

At the sound of my voice and the familiar smell of his mother, Andrew began to squirm and whimper to be fed.

Jillian helped me to expose a breast from my robe, and I placed Andrew's little mouth to it. He began to suckle deeply as if he was starving. I pulled his mouth away and was overjoyed to see milk run down the corner of his mouth. Putting him back to his meal, I rejoiced and praised God for His wonderful healing touch. Jillian smiled and left the room to allow us this precious time of mother and child alone together.

"She is feeding the baby." Jillian informed those still waiting outside, "My job here is done, and I have to walk to Gretchen's tent and let her know that she need not come by this evening to feed Andrew."

Mathias and the children looked at Asher with a puzzled look on their faces. Jillian laughed and said, "I see that you have told them nothing about what happened? I will go now and leave your company, while you find the words to explain all this." She smiled and started to leave but Mathias stood and asked to escort her, which she gladly accepted.

Mathias started his job of seed scattering right away as he walked with Jillian and told her about the meetings being held each evening. His excitement grew with each thought shared with Jillian. By the time they returned back to Jillian's tent, she had committed to attending the meetings. Mathias bowed low before her and walked back to our dwelling.

When Mathias returned, Luke was sitting on a stool thumping his finger against the hide of the seat which gave off a dull sound.

"Father is inside with Mama," he announced to Mathias without looking up. "Father instructed me to wait here for you so I could help you fetch the evening quail. He is spending time with Mama because she has had a hard day. That's what he told me, and so here I am."

"Yes, here you are." Mathias answered, "And when an Elder comes into your presence, young Israelite, you will stand on your feet and show respect to that elder. You will not merely acknowledge his or her presence nor will you simply sit there on your hind end and speak. You will stand to your feet and show the respect due that elder by bowing in courtesy before him or her. Do you understand this, young man?"

Luke jumped to his feet and quickly bowed himself before Mathias, and in turn, Mathias bowed before Luke.

"I know that times are changing in the day we live in, little man, but the old ways have been proven to be the best ways," Mathias told Luke as he sat down.

Luke did not sit down again until Mathias was comfortably seated.

"That is the way to think Luke. Always consider the other person to be of higher respect than yourself and show hospitality to all people when it is in your power to do so," Mathias continued.

"Good manners do not come naturally, but good habits can be practiced until they become good manners. Neither one will ever go out of fashion no matter how grown you may be. You must not judge yourself by what someone says about you or does to you. You must know within your own heart what manner of man you are, and it is high time that you began to practice all of this. Can you understand my meaning?"

Luke quickly nodded his head in agreement that he understood. He continued to watch Mathias waiting to see if the elder was going to say anything more. Luke began to search his own thoughts to have something intelligent to say, but decided to stay still lest he sound like a small child to the old man. Mathias waited for a while and spoke again to him.

"Now in the matter of your parents! You are to show admiration and love to them at all times even if you had the misfortune to be swatted for some bad behavior that caused it. You did apologize to your Mother today for the way you acted toward her. That is good and acceptable. But you should have never let your feelings of what others might think, cause you to disrespect her in the first place. She had done the wisest thing possible to help you when those boys had you on the ground kicking you. Yes, you were angry at the time of the incident, but never lose control of yourself because of your temper which could cause you more problems."

Mathias finished his oration and rose up. Immediately, Luke also jumped to his feet and stood before Mathias waiting to see if there was more to hear. Mathias chuckled and shifted his weight from one foot to the other before speaking again. Looking up at the old man made Luke feel like a small grasshopper, but he intended to stand there until he was dismissed by Mathias.

"Come and let us gather wood for the fire, and, when that has been done, the quail will begin to gather up for us to collect for the evening meal, my son," he said, turning about looking for Astoria.

"Where is your sister? Is she inside with your parents?"

Shaking his head no, Luke was quick to remember the old man's words, and so he spoke out and said, "No, my lord, she is not inside."

Making a quick bow before Mathias, Luke ran around to the back of the tent to see if Astoria was there. Mathias began to build up cross sections of wood in the fireplace as he waited for the children.

"Asher?" Mathias called out after a short look around the tent failed to locate Astoria's whereabouts. "It is necessary to speak with you."

Chapter 7

Mathias and Luke stood waiting for Asher to appear, and Mathias began wringing his hands together. Luke looked up at him as fear began to well up inside him. Asher came through the door opening shielding his eyes from the brightness of the outdoors. Mathias put his hand on Asher's shoulder and led him away from the tent door so Leeanna would not hear what was said.

"Astoria is missing, Asher. We have searched around the tent, and if she isn't inside the tent, then she is gone," Mathias said, with hope that Asher would tell him that she was inside the tent.

By the look on Asher's face, Mathias knew the answer. All the color drained from Asher's face as he heard this report.

"She is not inside Mathias. She was in front with Luke when I went in to be with Leeanna. Luke, did she tell you where she was going, or did you see her leave the area?"

"No Papa, I haven't seen her since after you went inside the tent. I was playing Marbles on the side there," Luke said, pointing to the side of the tent.

"She didn't follow you and Jillian, did she?" Asher turned looking at Mathias.

He knew the answer to that already because she was there with Luke in front of the tent just before he went inside to see about Leeanna. Mathias started toward his tent to retrieve his walking stick which he carried to prod the herd when they would not follow him.

"No Asher, she didn't follow me, and I will be right back as soon as I get my cattle prodder which I might have to use on a few belligerent men as we search for Astoria," he answered.

"Astoria, Astoria!" Luke called out loudly, "Where are you? Astoria, don't try to hide like when we play a game. Father is looking for you. Astoria, come on out! It is not a game this time!" Luke continued walking, cupping his hands to his mouth as he called out for Astoria.

Several people who were sitting or working in front of their tents came out to ask Asher what was the trouble. After Asher informed them of why they had been shouting, others joined in and helped search for the child, too. A missing child, no matter what else may be happening at any time, was a grave situation, and everyone young and old was ready to help. After all, it could be your child missing, and every parent felt it was their own personal grief.

An audible gasp went through the crowd of gathered people as Mathias approached carrying the small, limp body in his arms. As they made way for him to pass, Asher saw Mathias, and dropped to his knees shaking his head.

"Oh my God, no!" he screamed into the sky. "Why did you take my little girl from me?"

"The child is alive, Asher! She is still alive!" Mathias called out to him.

Asher scrambled up from his knees and ran over to Mathias. Mathias quickly told him that her breath was still in her, but he had seen vomit alongside her hair when he turned her over. There were a few, small purple berries in the vomit, and he picked them up to see if he could determine what they were.

An old woman in the crowd pushed her way through and told Mathias to give the berries to her. She would be able to tell him what kind they were and what to do if the berries had caused this to Astoria. Asher nodded his head toward the old woman and told Mathias to give them to her. Asher took the child from Mathias's arms. He turned toward our tent to take Astoria there.

"Give the child to me. I know what to do for her. These berries will make her very sick but the child will not die," the old woman said as Asher turned back toward her.

A younger woman stepped forward and received Astoria from Asher's arms.

"She will be fine in our care, my lord. My mother may be old, but she knows the herbs better than she knows her name at times. The child will be safe with us, and we will help her get rid of this poison in her stomach. She will be returned to you as soon as Mother thinks it is good for her. Our dwelling is just beyond you to the right where the blue and white scarf is attached to the pole," she said pointing her finger in that direction.

Several people standing there gave their assurance to Asher that was true. The crowd made room once again for the old woman and her daughter to pass. Asher watched as the two women entered their tent. Then he turned to the crowd and thanked them for their assistance in searching for his daughter.

Asher looked over at Mathias and walked up to him as the crowd began to thin out. Mathias informed him that he had heard a noise in his tent when he went to get his prodding stick. Upon entering, he found Astoria curled up on his bed. As he reached down to shake her from sleep, he found the vomit along the side of her hair and realized she was very sick.

"The rest of it you know," he told Asher.

Chapter 8

The arguing had gone on for hours. Various heated voices were shouting about taking matters into their own hands and returning to Egypt. Others were arguing to persuade against this detrimental decision. Groups for each side were vying to persuade the others to agree with their argument. The continued debate had nerve-wracking, tense moments until both groups were exhausted from their efforts. The shouts had escalated at times to severe blows passed between the groups, as if blows would bring any agreement.

As the hours passed, most of the men grew weary and began to slip quietly away from the groups. They had stood before Aaron from midday through the late afternoon, and no one had eaten anything during this time. As the time grew near for the evening quail to appear atop the land, the men left off their heated debate before Aaron. Before returning to their tents, they promised each other another round of the same come morning.

Elder Jarrod, the one who had spoken with Asher earlier in the day, felt a mood of despair envelop him along with total exhaustion in his body. His group had stood the test with every argument presented, and, for this, he was grateful. But because of his own great age, he had come to know a lot about the hearts and whims of mankind. The dejection he felt was apparent as his shoulders sagged with exhaustion. He knew in his heart that time alone with God was his immediate intention upon arriving back to his own tent.

The group who was debating alongside Elder Jarrod walked with him as they made their way back through the different camps. Finally Elder Jarrod stopped and turned around to face his companions with a sad look on his face. The other men waited to see what he was about to do. The old man stood looking tired and forlorn. They knew that this day, with all the tension and arguing, was a lot for the elder to bear at his age. As Elder Jarrod lifted up his face to the sky, his voice broke as he tried to call on God. His body crumbled to the ground, and his cries became so intense that all the other men fell onto the ground with him. A spirit of heart-wrenching prayer rose from each man.

The group stayed upon the ground for a long time, until the urgency of their hearts before God subsided. As each man stood up from prayer, he had the sense of rejuvenation throughout his entire body. The exhaustion, the sadness, the mood of despair, and the hurt feelings were all gone. All these had been replaced with renewed hope, renewed strength, renewed attitude, and renewed faith implanted in them from God. No longer were their feet dragging and their shoulders sagging. They felt as if they could spend three days in debates and not grow weary.

****

As Aaron escaped into the safety of his tent, his rapidly beating heart began to slow to a normal pace. The muscles in his face began to relax, but the tension in his body was causing painful muscle spasms. He looked around the interior of his tent for something or someway to ease this condition. Picking up his cup to pour himself some milk, he suddenly threw the cup with all his might against the wall of the tent. Next he picked up a stool and hurled it against the wall as hot scalding tears streamed down his tired face.

"What manner of man am I?" he shouted to the empty tent. "Why do I cower before these men with my legs barely holding me up? I did not ask for this burden nor do I want it! Where is my brother, Moses? He was given the task of leading all these people, not me! I am barely able to control the shaking of my hands and the trembling of my knees as I stand before these stiff-necked people. My life is in danger at every moment and at every turn! Let someone else take this burden and allow me to hide my shamefulness away from Your eyes! Give Your call to Hur or to another of Your choosing, but do not call me to carry on with this dangerous task anymore! I cannot stand before these men and not feel fear! I am not Moses! I am only his brother, and I ask You, am I my brother's keeper? My shame is more than I can bear! Let me go and return Moses to the people. He is their leader, not me!"

Aaron fell exhausted onto his sleeping mat and cried himself into a restless sleep.

****

After listening to the report Asher gave concerning the trial with that group of renegades, one can certainly sympathize with Aaron's fears. I suppose it takes a special breed of man to take hold of some task in life and not waver at one time or another. My thought was that Aaron was no different.

When we first heard of Moses back in Egypt before we were rescued, he lived in Pharaoh's palace. The Israelites knew about his heritage because his parents were of Hebrew descent. Pharaoh had become afraid about the increase of Hebrew people and thought the Hebrews might rise up and take over his kingdom. Pharaoh ordered the slaying of all infant Hebrew males, thinking that act would eventually decrease the population of the Hebrews. There was one Hebrew family who hid their son away to prevent his death by Pharaoh's soldiers. The baby had been placed in a basket woven from reeds and put out to float in the Nile River with his fate trusted to the care of God. The daughter of Pharaoh spotted the basket floating in some reeds and had it brought to her. Inside the basket laid the baby who was unharmed and healthy. The sure sign of his heritage was obvious by his circumcision.

The princess loved the baby right away and called for a wet nurse to nurse the child and a certain price was set for payment. The baby's sister, Marion, had been standing by watching all these proceedings, and she came forward informing the princess of such a woman who would nurse the baby. The young girl had secured the task with her own mother in mind, which was the baby's mother. The arrangements were made, and baby Moses was allowed to be nursed by his own mother. His sister Marion, had been the instrument God had used.

After the child was weaned from the breast of his mother, he was brought to the princess at Pharaoh's palace to live. Moses grew and became knowledgeable in all manner of learning which was taught by tutors. He knew he was the son of Hebrew parents, and one day decided to go forth to observe the work the Hebrew slaves were doing. When he saw one of his own people of Hebrew decent being beaten by an Egyptian taskmaster, Moses intervened and killed the offender. Moses, the young child, had grown into a great man during his days at Pharaoh's court, but his deed was found out and he had to flee for his life to escape the hand of Pharaoh.

Moses lived in the wilderness of Midian for forty years. He married a woman from Midian, and they produced two sons from that marriage. His life was peaceful as a sheep herder until he was called one day to tend God's sheep, the people of Israel, the Hebrews, who were yet enslaved in Egypt. God appointed Moses to go to Pharaoh to secure deliverance for Israel.

After God caused many awesome plagues to come on the Egyptians, the Israelites were released. My family is one of thousands rescued who are waiting for Moses to return from the mountain to once again lead God's people in the same manner as one leads sheep. We are God's sheep, and Moses was given the task of being God's voice to the people, but God is indeed the Shepherd of us all.

****

Even with all that was happening in the camps of Israel, still God's gracious bounty continued. He is such a gracious and merciful God, full of kindness and love for everyone.

While listening to my parents about the stories of the forefathers, I remember having such a warm feeling that rose up inside of me. It was like Someone unseen had wrapped His arms around me. I so regretted it when time came to let the stories rest until we could once again gather at Father's feet to listen and learn.

My father always used any chance or opportunity he could to assimilate areas of everyday life to the advantage of teaching his children with God's truth. There are times even now that I long to sit and hear his gentle voice make these stories come to life before my very eyes and heart.

Chapter 9

"Do you know from where Astoria got the berries she ate Luke?" Mathias asked Luke as they walked back to the tent.

Luke's heart began beating very fast. He knew he was the cause of his sisters' illness and thought that Mathias could see it in his face. Luke had suddenly developed a quick respect for the old man, and he was sure that Mathias was able to guess whatever was in his thoughts. When he had gone out to help Mathias with milking or fetching water, it seemed the old man would always answer Luke's questions before he could ask them. Luke wasn't sure if his thought was true, but he never seemed to get by the old man on anything he did. Mathias stopped and turned Luke around to face him. Placing his hand beneath Luke's chin, Mathias lifted the boys face up so he could watch his reaction as he asked the question again. Luke's lips began to tremble, and he slowly nodded his head yes.

Then he quickly remembered what Mathias had said to him earlier about respecting one's elders, and so he followed the head nod with a quiet "Yes, my lord, I do know."

He couldn't help but cry as he told Mathias how Astoria had come to eat the berries.

"It was my fault. She kept pestering me everyday wanting to know how to be strong and jump high and climb on those dumb rocks. I tried to tell her that she was just a silly old girl, and girls do not wrestle and climb on rocks. They just sit around and play with their hair and with drawing sticks and giggle a lot. Then one day, a baby comes out, and they have to stop playing games and take care of the baby."

"Those silly girls try to be like us boys, running and jumping and climbing. But when one of them falls down off a rock, she cries and screams like she might die. When I gave those berries to her, I hoped with all my heart that it would really work for her and make her big and strong so she would leave me and the boys alone," he confessed, while Mathias couldn't help but chuckle behind his hand.

"I am very proud of you little Israelite for telling me the truth about what happened, but I am also very disappointed at you for thinking up such a scheme to play on your sister. Anytime you have such a problem where you can't find a solution for it, why do you not just seek out someone to ask advice from? Two heads are better than one head unless one of the heads is empty and has nothing inside but pebbles rolling around in it. When you are young, lots of times you will need some answers for your questions and problems. You need to seek out someone who is wise and has shown them self to be a friend and a person you can trust, a person like your father, mother, and even this old man," Mathias said, pointing to his own chest. "Now we both know that when your parents hear that it was your idea to give those berries to your sister that you are in for a large punishment, do we not?"

Luke quickly dropped his head down but remembered to answer Mathias instead of merely nodding his head.

"Yes, my lord, we both know that is true," he answered.

"Then prepare yourself to take the punishment you deserve like a true Israelite, and have no fear, but learn the reason for it well, my son." Mathias said, as they began walking toward the tent, the place which Luke thought would be his certain doom.

Mathias knew just how the boy must feel. Luke had gone through many emotions in his little body today and was still facing a confession to his parents.

"Life is rough," he thought, as the two of them walked along, "but one has to deal with what has been put on his plate, and, in this case, what one puts on his own plate."

Mathias continued his thought, "I know the boy needs punishment of some sort, but I hope his father will listen to him with not only his ears but with his heart also. There is some understanding to Luke's admission as to why he gave Astoria the berries, but, again, he knew he was lying to her about the results she could expect from eating them."

"O dear Lord of mercy," he prayed silently, "our lives do indeed resemble a wilderness as we plough through each day with all of its sorrows, problems, joys, and deaths. O how we do need to learn to handle each day with its thorns a plenty, but without experiencing the sorrows and disappointments, we could never fully appreciate the joys."

"And dear Lord," he prayed as his thoughts floated back in times past, "if I had my entire life to live over again, if I had that choice, I wouldn't want to live it again. No, not in the least! You and Ihave come down these dusty roads, and, as we walked, You taught me something more valuable than life itself. You have proven to this old heart that there is One Who is closer than a brother, and each step we take brings this old man closer to the finish line where he will see that One, face to face. I have, in my life, experienced hard labor, enough to last me the rest of my days, but not too much that it laid me down in the grave. I have had times when my stomach was empty as that bird nest in the bush, but also times when my stomach was full and my sleep sweet; times when I was blessed with holding my baby in my arms, and a time when I laid her down in the grave. There were times when I rejoiced with my loving wife and times when we held each other and cried. I've had times when friends were abundant and now times when friends are few. There were times when the wolf was howling at my door and times when my coin pouch was full. There were times when a kind word was spoken to me in my pain and times when cursing has beaten me down. I have had times of shadows on the walls of my mind and times when Your voice drove them away, times when my tongue would cling to my cheek, and times when it wagged uncontrolled. There were times of falling at Your feet in despair and times when hope flooded my soul. What price would one pay for such abundance dear Lord? What price indeed?" He prayed fervently as they walked along

"I wonder what Father is going to do to me, my lord?" Luke spoke up and brought Mathias' thoughts back to his dilemma. "I am almost as afraid as I was that time when I was caught between a rock and a hard place with a snake watching me to see what I was going to do. I had to think fast so he wouldn't know. I stood up as tall as I could stretch and just swung my arms from side to side while he was watching me. I tried to fool him, though, because he thought I was going to jump down off that rock, and he planned to run over there and bite me. But I didn't jump. I just stood there and swung my arms so that pretty soon he got tired of watching and crawled away. I was sure scared, but he was sure tired," Luke confessed as they arrived at his door.

Mathias had purposely lagged behind Asher to give him time to let me know about Astoria.

"She is in good hands Leeanna," he said after telling me the whole affair.

"Dear Lord," I replied, getting to my feet, "what else will this day bring on this family?"

After asking which tent our daughter was in, I put the baby in his arms and started out the door.

"Stay here, stay right here, and do not go anywhere," I said to Luke in passing, as he was approaching the tent with Mathias.

Luke tugged on Mathias's sleeve and looking up at him, he said, "I know it is going to be bad, very bad for me."

Mathias knew where I was going and did not make a move to stop me. It is a wise man who knows not to come between a mother and the safety of her children. I knew he was watching me as I hurried to the tent of the old woman and her daughter.

"Thank You, God, that you always have an angel of mercy somewhere close in times of need," I prayed.

Gretchen greeted me at the tent door after I called out 'hello.' I explained that I was Astoria's Mother and had come as soon as I heard. I was relieved to see Gretchen and was not aware that it was her mother whom Asher had told me about.

"Come in Leeanna." Gretchen said, "Your daughter is in good hands. Mother has given her an herbal dose to make her vomit and rid her stomach of the poisonous berries. Astoria is still very sick, but she will be better in a few hours. Come, she is awake, but soon she will take the heaves and will be wishing she could sleep. Of course, we will not allow her to sleep until we are sure the poison is all gone."

Astoria's face had a pale color, and a touch on her arm showed that she was fevered. Gretchen's mother stood over Astoria with a wet cloth and replaced the one from her forehead with the fresh cloth. There was a bowl setting beside Astoria ready for use when necessary. I felt I had to explain to the two women, why I had not come sooner. But the older woman held up her hand and told me that they knew already. Jillian had stopped by earlier to let Gretchen know that I would not need her. All that was left to do now was to wait for the herbs to begin their work, and soon there would be plenty for us to do.

I offered my deepest appreciation and Gretchen made us a cup of warm milk while we waited and tended to Astoria. Soon it was all over with, and I was able to take my daughter home. She was still weak, but, praise God, she was still alive.

Chapter 10

"Leeanna and I will not be attending the meeting tonight," Asher said to Mathias as they were waiting for my return to see about my daughter. "This day has brought to our family many trials and tribulations. I think it is best that we remain here in our dwelling tonight and take our rest from the many things that brought us to the point of despair. We are all exhausted in mind and body, and we wait to see how Astoria will fare from her illness."

"That is a good plan, my son," Mathias replied as he sat before his young friend. "The weight of this day shows in your face, and your speech has the sound of despair. A good night's rest will do you a world of good, and, with God's help, tomorrow will be a better day. If you have no objection, I ask if you will allow Luke to come to the meeting with me? I will take proper care of him and will see to it that he keeps silent and stays beside me at all times."

On returning to the tent after the episode of finding Astoria, Luke had taken it upon himself to confess before his Father the part he played in Astoria eating the poison berries. Naturally, Asher became angry and scolded Luke for some time. He was told that his punishment would be decided on after being discussed with his mother. Though Asher was angry with Luke for deceiving his sister with the berries, deep within his heart, there was planted a seed of respect for the boy's honesty and courage. Asher had watched Luke as the boy confessed his deed, and Luke continued to look over at Mathias as if he gained some encouragement from him. After Asher had given his rebuke to Luke about the tragedy that could have happened, he sent him inside. Asher watched as Mathias wiped away tears from his own eyes, and a smile spread across the elder's face as he turned his back to Asher. But then turned and faced him again.

"May God be praised!" Asher heard him say. "This young Israelite stood before the lion of fright and anger but kept his honor in tact! A mighty man shall he make and one who knows the value of taking what is his due in the face of God and man! An honest heart supports the gift of courage! There are many years to spend teaching this young boy, and it would honor me if I could be allowed a part of them."

Asher had no idea that the old man had such feelings about children, but then Mathias had always been ready to help in anything. According to Asher's parents, there was a time when anyone's children in the tribes of Israel were considered to be a concern for all. All the people were willing and were expected to participate in the rearing of a child, especially the male children. All manner of learning came as a result from various ones.

"But of course! You may take him with you this evening, my friend," Asher answered. "I cannot think of another person who I would trust with my son as well as I trust you."

Asher was truly beginning to see different areas to this blessed friendship with Mathias, and he was grateful for Luke to be exposed to such a one.

"The quail are beginning to descend upon the outer parts of the camps, and, if we expect to have a meal this evening, we had best be about gathering it," Mathias stated as he stood looking out toward the mountain.

Mathias reached for the net he had made from twisting goats' hair into long strips and weaving them around a hoop made from reeds. He attached a long pole made from small branches tied together at various intervals with more goats' hair strips. Mathias would carry the basket to put the quail in, and it would be Asher's job to trap them in the net. Asher called to Luke from the door of the tent and told him to come along with them to help. Luke was glad to hear that he was allowed to go with the two men because gathering the birds was a lot of fun to him.

Along the way, Mathias thought about a teaching he learned from the Lord while gathering the quail for the evening meal.

"The meat of God's Word does not fall out of the sky like these birds. Nor does it just appear in your heart as these birds appear on the ground. It takes effort and work from a person to gather these birds; it takes preparing yourself with the proper tools to gather them. It takes your steadfastness and your energy to gather them. When you have been fortunate to have caught them, the work continues. It does not cease simply because you have a few birds in your basket. Now you must prepare the birds and prepare the water to scald its body so the feathers can be plucked easily."

"After the meat has been prepared in this way, then you must cook it thoroughly. You do not simply swallow it whole for where then, is the flavor for your enjoyment? You must chew the meat and gnaw all the tiny bits from the bones. When the meat is swallowed, then your stomach begins to feel relief from its hunger. Your life is sustained as your belly becomes satisfied with this delicious meat. So in like manner is the Word of God. It is food indeed for your heart and soul. But this meat does not just fall from the sky for your enjoyment. Neither will one time of feasting on this Word last you for the rest of your days. When you hear the Word, you must listen with the tools God has given you: your ears, your heart, your eyes, your speech, and your understanding. All these tools are necessary for it's inception within you. There is work here, also, in one's energy and steadfastness to gather the Word in your heart. You must be faithful to set yourself against your own desires and practice these truths. Prepare your heart to receive the Word of God. Always be diligent to remind yourself that your heart needs to have good soil to plant the Word into. The Words will cause you to feel the heat of the truth and assist you in weeding out the things which are not good in your heart. Next you must study these truths over and over again as one would chew meat before swallowing it. When you chew on the meat of these truths, the flavor and goodness begins to satisfy your taste. Let these truths be active in all areas of your life. Be hungry to gnaw every tiny morsel of delicious truth from others who are willing to share and to listen to God's Word. You must allow it to multiply and grow, being full of good truths. In doing all these things, you are sustained and satisfied in your heart, in your mind, in your strength, and in your life. There will always be an Amalekite that will attack you at times in your weakest areas. Some of these enemies come from your own heart and thoughts, but the Word of God in you will lift up a standard against them. Just as Moses lifted up his staff against the Amalekites, you must lift up God's Word as a standard against these enemies which taunt and pinch you, threaten you, and try to cause you to fail. Your life will indeed be one battle after another, but you must stand on God's Word. So guard the Word of God which is in you. It is life's anchor."

Now every time Mathias went out to gather quail, he could not help but think on what God had shown him through this activity. He remembered that Luke was with them and how much fun the boy had each time he came.

"I will try to teach Luke what I have learned from God so perhaps he, too, will further enjoy this trip to gather the birds as I do," he thought.

The men busied themselves with netting the birds, and Luke was a big help to them both. In only a short time, all three returned to our dwelling to begin the process of cleaning the birds for our meal. Astoria was still a little sick to her stomach, but I knew she would be fine after a good nights rest. I planned to question her in the morning to determine how she came to eat the berries. It was no use at this time to question her. Neither she nor I had the strength to go through it now. I am only grateful to God that she is still with us.

After we finished the evening meal, Mathias and Luke departed to attend the group meeting taking place at Elder Jarrod's dwelling. Asher helped me clean the dishes, and then we sat down for a talk. The day had been long and full of all manner of events. We were both exhausted in mind and body. Asher picked up Andrew and played with him for some time before giving him to me so he could be changed and fed before time for sleep. I was grateful for his kindness in helping me because my strength was almost gone. Every move I made took extra effort, and that extra supply was almost depleted.

As I fed the baby, Asher told me about Luke's confession concerning the berries. We discussed what manner of punishment to give him and agreed that Astoria also should shoulder some punishment for her part. Asher watched my face as I stood to go inside and put the baby down for the night.

"I will wait up for Luke and Mathias to return," he said. "You should lie down, too, Leeanna. God only knows what tomorrow will bring. Perhaps Mathias will tell us the messages he and Luke heard in the morning."

On their return, Mathias appeared worried as he and Luke greeted Asher. Asher was alarmed to see his friend's look of worry pulling at the corners of his mouth and the skin of his brow was creased. After a few words with Luke, Asher sent the child to bed so they could talk. Mathias sat down heavily on a stool with his hands upon his knees as he waited for Luke to go inside. Asher pulled his stool closer to Mathias so they could lower their voices as they talked. Taking a deep breath Mathias looked into Asher's eyes and began to speak.

"There is going to be a decision made tomorrow one way or the other," he said. "Jarrod and the other men are returning in the morning to again confront those who are stirring up the people to return to Egypt. If the contention is as severe as it was today, with arguing and fighting amongst the groups, then it is Jarrod's plan to let those who desire to turn back to Egypt, return, and he will not stand in the way. Aaron has tried very little to lessen their dissension and tends to listen to their arguments without comment. Fear of the group appears to be in him."

Mathias finished speaking and waited for Asher's reply.

"Leeanna will have a full night's rest tonight, and perhaps she and Luke will be able to collect the morning manna," Asher said. "If you agree, you and I will join Jarrod's group at Aaron's tent. We will try to bring a united force against this spirit of fear which has found ground to plant its wicked seed into. I pray God's mercy be upon those who have given place to this weed of destruction."

Chapter 11

"**If** God, be God, then let Him contend for Himself. Why is there no sign of His presence? We have the Words He gave to Moses here with us. Are they not written in a book to give us direction? Perhaps this is all He intends to do with us and has given us leave to return to Egypt and serve Him there," Amadeus shouts to the people gathered before him that morning. "Were there not any graves in Egypt that He would bring this great people out to a wilderness just to destroy us? Our ancestors have, for over four hundred years, died and were laid to rest in that mighty land. Their graves are there still," he took a deep breath. "The entire multitude which stands here this day was born in that land, and it is our tradition to be laid to rest beside our fathers. God did not bring us here to this barren place to kill us, O Israel. He brought us here to give us His terms of worship and the practice of the way He desires to be served. Whether it be here or in Egypt matters not to Him. Do we see any prison bars across our path or any armed soldiers guarding us from returning? Let us make a god which will go triumphal before us, back to our place of birth. We will show all who see our entry that Israel has her own god, and he marches with her!"

He began waving a banner back and forth, and another in the crowd blew on a horn. The people started shouting, and there were more kerchiefs waved in the air as the noise of the crowd grew to a deafening pitch. There was no place given for Jarrod's group to have their say. Many of them ran into the fever-pitched crowd to confront them, but no one would tolerate listening to their words. The men were pushed and shoved until Jarrod's group, including Asher and Mathias, were squeezed to the back of the shouting mob. Jarrod's group formed together again after being shoved outside the arena of shouting men. Jarrod made a very profound statement to them.

"Having ears to hear, yet they hear not. May their desires be a snare to them because their hearts have become dark and hardened, and their eyes have become blind."

The fervor of the crowd began to ebb as they saw Aaron standing on a rock with his arms raised toward them for silence.

"If this is your desire to return to Egypt, then so be it," he told the waiting crowd of men.

At once the roar of the crowd and waving of kerchiefs began again. Aaron waved his arms back and forth to cause silence.

As they grew silent, Amadeus shouted to Aaron, "Build us a god that will go before us, build us a god that will go before us, build us a god that will go before us," he continued shouting until the crowd picked up the chant with him.

Again waving his arms for silence, Aaron tells the crowd, "Break off the gold earrings from your wives and children and bring the earrings to me. I will build you a god and cover it with the gold from your ears, O Israel. As for your leader Moses, I do not know what has become of him, but we do have the words here with us that God spoke to him. Perhaps something has befallen him. The days have grown into many since he ascended the mountain into God's presence. I have no words from God to share with you, but God has continued to bless Israel with the manna and quail every day. I have tried to shoulder the responsibility of this great multitude since Moses' departure, and I have grown weary with the worry of you all. The last word from Moses to me and the elders was for us to remain until his return to the camp. We all saw the frightening display upon the top of Mt. Sinai and heard the thunder. We felt the ground quake beneath our feet, and so you asked Moses to let God not speak to us again. The elders and I saw the beautiful pavement beneath the feet of the Lord when we were upon the mountain, and He did not harm us. How can you then ask me to fashion a god in likeness of Him? Who among you could fashion such a one as majestic as He, or what likeness would be suitable for His glory?"

Aaron argued, trying to stave off their blasphemous suggestions.

"There is no room for error with this mighty God. He is One who makes water run in abundant supply from the flinty rock to quench our thirst. He brought great and awesome plagues upon the Egyptians when Pharaoh's heart remained stubborn. Do you, indeed, plan a revolt against such a One as He who is able to crush us with his hand? How do we worship and bless Him in all this you have planned? Has it been such a long time since you were in slavery that the horror of your captivity has faded? Our people were in Egypt for over four hundred years, and that land is all we have known. But God sent a deliverer through Moses to set us free. If Moses does not return to us from the mountain, then God will raise up another leader, perhaps from amongst you, to lead us. I am not my brother, and I have no desire to step into his shoes as leader of this multitude. If indeed you continue on in this plan to return to Egypt knowing what you will find there, then you may do so, but the blood of your wives and children will be upon your hands," Aaron shouts, as the embittered crowd begins chanting against his advice.

Aaron desperately looked around for the elders who had been with him on the mountain, who had experienced God's presence as he had. He could see some of them huddled together in small groups, whispering to one another, but no one came to his aid.

The air above Aaron's body seemed to be alive with a tingling fear that crept up his legs and threatened to take over his body. The roar of the crowd became deafening, and his weak knees began to buckle beneath his frame. He had never known such a feeling of fear and sensed that his life would be in jeopardy if he continued to debate the crowd. All that was left was to let the people have their way, and if he did not assist them in making this god, he felt he might not live through the rest of the day.

Asher, Mathias, and Jarrod's group slowly began to return to their own dwelling. What Aaron had said gave each one of them a sense of impending doom. The men knew they could not fight their brothers or persuade them that their foolish plans could lead to death for the entire nation of Israel. They felt as though some awful omen of disaster would come with the completion of this god Aaron was to fashion at the demands of those wicked men. Where was God? How could He allow this dreadful thing to continue in Israel? Could he not see what was happening, and could He not hear the slanderous words spoken by this group of dissenters? Does He not care or is He too busy to rouse Himself and investigate this turmoil?

Chatting amongst themselves in these avenues of thought gave them something to mull over in their own hearts and minds. What if Amadeus's group was right, and God had completed His task for Israel? Maybe He had finished His commands to the people and expected them to return to Egypt but continue worshipping Him there. Surely there is no reason to stay here in this barren wilderness, and there are numerous places we can go to where we will not be in danger of captivity again. How much longer will God continue to supply food and water for us here? This is an inhospitable place for dwelling over long periods of time, they reasoned among themselves.

Asher arrived at his tent and fell upon his mat in the coolness of the interior. The family was still out gathering manna, and Mathias had retired to his own tent. As he lay there and contemplated his own thoughts, his mind reeled with the morning's events. He remembered hearing voices just beyond the tent door as he drifted into sleep.

"Your father is sleeping," I informed the children, dropping the tent flap back into its place. "Astoria, you may sit here and tend to Andrew while I prepare a meal. I am sure everyone is hungry, and Luke, you may stoke the fire and build it up while I grind the manna for pancakes."

"Yes Mama," was their concerted reply.

The events of yesterday had taken a toll on our family. No one had done their daily chores. There was much to get done today, and soon things would return to normal, I thought, as I busied myself with cooking. I tried to keep my thoughts on the task at hand and away from the questions I wanted to ask Asher concerning the early morning meeting the men had with Aaron. I felt secure in my heart that Asher and Mathias were able to talk sense into the group of men who were parading their poisonous speeches around the camp. Somewhere deep inside me came a sense of fear that our lives were about to change. My hands began to tremble as I placed the pancakes on a platter and heated honey over the fire to pour on them.

****

"Things have gone a lot further than I thought," Asher said, as he dipped the pancake into the warm honey.

Swirling the cake around in the honey, he drifted off into deep thoughts. I waited patiently for him to continue talking, so I refilled his cup with milk as he finished eating. My thoughts were like hands grasping my mind as I waited to hear more from my husband. I had awaked him so he could join us in the meal. Asher waited until the children were about their chores to begin this talk.

"Some of the words the Amadeus group said are very interesting," Asher said. "I have also listened closely to the words Aaron said today."

Asher looked at me as he talked, but his thoughts were more reflected in his eyes as he weighed out every word he said. Dropping his gaze and spreading his hands on his knees, he continued.

"Could it be that they are right in what they have determined to do?"

He asked the question but desired no answer for it. My heart skipped a beat as I watched and listened to my husband saying these strange things, and I was not sure that I wanted him to continue.

"Why do you say such things Asher?" I questioned him. "How could you possibly succumb to their lies when only this morning you were set to rebuke them?"

My eyes were filling with tears of frustration, and I felt fear grip at my heart like briars. Brushing away the tears which ran down my face, I leaned toward him and caused him to look at me again.

"You must explain to me why you are simply giving up and reducing all we have stood for to nothing but ashes!" I whispered frantically through clenched teeth.

"I am not giving up at all. I am simply looking at this whole thing in a different way, Leeanna. Perhaps we have fought against God and what He wants us to do. Since the disappearance of Moses, this whole multitude has wondered what is to become of us. These people are not our enemies, Leeanna, but they are our brethren and are trying to figure out what the next step should be for Israel," he said, as I stared at him with my mouth open in disbelief.

"They are not "all brethren" who came out with us from Egypt, Asher," I replied. "The leader, Amadeus, is not Israeli at all! If he wants to go back to Egypt, then let him go and leave us in peace! It is for sure, he and his group have brought much chaos to our people."

"If you want me to tell you all about what took place at the meeting, Leeanna, then you must keep quiet and allow me to talk," he said between tight lips.

The very tone of his voice was beginning to change toward me, and I could feel fear tighten its grip on my heart. I sat and waited for him to continue and decided to delay any questions I had until he finished. I could see that Asher struggled with every word he said. It was as if the struggle inside him fought to be heard.

"Today I heard a different view come from Amadeus about our being here in this place and God's dealings with us," Asher said. "As Mathias and I walked back from the meeting, we discussed many of the possibilities we heard as to where we stand here in this wilderness and with God. Could it be that God has ended the migration of Israel here in this barren place and wants us to continue in His word no matter where we decide to go from here? Perhaps He raised someone already from amongst those different men to take the place of Moses. Perhaps today He caused their voice to be heard concerning our destiny. God continues to feed and water us as He did before Moses left. But how long will He be gracious in this while we argue and fight for the right to stay

when He might want us to leave? We have His written oracle in a book
Moses wrote before he departed to go back up to God on the mountain
top," he continued, after drawing air into his lungs.

"Why do we stay here and continue to wait for Moses to return
when perhaps God has completed His call on Moses' life concerning our
deliverance? The people are weary and restless with waiting and are
pining to settle down once again wherever each family desires to settle.
We can take God with us where we decide to settle, and if it is not
Egypt, then somewhere else. There has been no word from God since
that day He spoke to us from the mountaintop, and it may be that He is
providing and sustaining us with food and water until we go on to
wherever we will go," Asher finished speaking and looked out toward
the mountain, as though there could be a sign to confirm his report.

I sat stunned in silence trying to put all these thoughts straight in
my mind. Where is Mathias, I wondered? What will he have to say in
regard to this way of thinking? As if reading my thoughts, Asher
informed me that Mathias had come to think along the same terms as he
had, and several of Jarrod's group agreed on it this morning. What? Am
I surrounded by lies even from my own husband and friend? Where has
their faith gone, and why are they giving in to this deception? I rose up
from my stool and began to pace back and forth, folding my arms across
my chest as waves of anger enveloped me. I have a lot of talking to do,
and Asher shall not stop me with his angry face again. He said we all
should think about this and ponder it over in our minds before coming to
a decision. Well, I have a lot of pondering to do, and it does not involve
agreeing with such foolishness. I am ready to fight for my belief, and,
after all is said and done, I will stand my ground by faith until God tells
me different. I will lift up the banner of the Lord, and, with His shield,
quench all the lying darts of fire that come against us, so help me Lord!

God surely did not bring this great company of people out here
to this wilderness to just give us a few words and then retreat back into
His heaven leaving us to migrate wherever each man decides is best.

Moses gave us the promises of God that we would be brought
into a land to call our own, a land full and abundant, a land flowing with
milk and honey, and this wilderness does not fit such a description. Our
people have endured extreme hardships and yet have multiplied in
number. Why, then, would we have left that horrid place in Egypt for
hopes of a better place for us if this wilderness was our destiny? There
are no grassy plains for our cattle to graze on, there are no trees laden
with different fruits, there are no fertile fields to plant crops, and there
are no rivers or streams flowing throughout for our water.

As I look around me at this barren place, I only see a place of decision. It is a barren place where there is no hope, yet I know on the other side there is a promise that God will faithfully fulfill. God gave us a glorious promise, but, in this place of decision, He waits to see if we will choose Him or choose to return to the old life by our own choice. We are not suffering here and are sustained by His mighty favor. He is testing our hearts for a period of time to see if we will follow Him willingly and wait on His direction. Each person must endure such a crossroad in their life whether it is to stay in the wilderness of their old life or willingly follow God in His promise of abundance in a new life. I want my children to have a life where they are free and able to thrive with God's help. Why would I hold tightly to a handful of cow dung when God has promised me fields with many cattle? Why tightly grasp a handful of sand when it slips through my fingers and soon there is little left when God has promised me a land flowing with milk and honey? Why would I throw away the olive and hold tightly to the pit when God has promised me trees full of fruit and a land to plant the olive pit? Why would I usurp my husbands' authority over our family decisions? Simply because he is being deceived, and his faith is on the road to destruction! Today is a good day for standing on the promises of God and not giving place to doubts or to what I see around me. If there is a battle to be won, then the only armor I need is God's promises and His favor. Let the battle be put in array for my heart is armed with the Word of God, and my voice will be my weapon of choice. I will speak and rehearse in Asher's ears about the solid ground of promise we must stand on. The same promise that was given to us by God, our faithful redeemer.

****

Chapter 12

"Look Luke," Astoria said, while they went about their chores, "I am not bigger or stronger like you told me I would be. Why did you taunt me into thinking those berries would give me what I desired? All they did was made me sick and weak in my body."

"You were the one who kept pestering me everyday to show you a secret way to get what you wanted," Luke answered her. "I am not God, Astoria, and, because of your own silly desires, you fell victim to a great big lie. You are what God made you to be, and nothing anyone can say or do will change that. Most girls go around primping their hair and giggling at the boys all day, but you want to be different. You want to be like the boys. One day you will be a grown woman just like Mama and maybe have a lot of children to tend to. Do you want to throw all that God has planned for your life away in exchange for strong arms to wrestle the boys or long legs so you can leap off an old rock? No man wants his wife and babies going around jumping off rocks all day. Don't you want a husband and babies like those old girls who giggle while they watch us boys in a wrestling contest? Why do you want to wrestle anyway? You will just get real dirty, and sometimes you get hurt when a head bangs into your mouth. Would you like to go around with a black eye and a cut lip with all that blood running down your chin for everyone to see?" Luke asked her as he pointed to each bruise on his body.

Luke could tell that the picture of horror he carefully painted was getting the effect he intended. Astoria's eyes grew bigger with everything Luke said, and she shrank back a step with each horrible thought.

She assumed that Luke knew all about things like this since he was all the time coming home with some new injury to his face or body. She did not know how much more blood was in his body for future wrestling contest because he had already lost a lot of it, and sometimes she would cry when helping him wipe it off. Astoria walked over to the water pot and peered into the water to see her reflection, trying to imagine what she would look like with black eyes and a cut lip. Luke watched her stare into the water for several minutes before he thought of something else to say that would help in her decision about wanting to be like the boys. Suddenly, he had a great idea. He smiled as his plan came into being in his mind, and, before he got weak kneed and quit the idea, he plunged forward with full speed and tackled Astoria from the side while her attention was on her reflection in the water.

"If she wants to be like a boy then I will show her what it feels like, so she will never want to be like one again," he thought, as he collided against her, sending them both sprawling across the rocky sand.

Astoria and Luke tumbled and rolled across the rocks and sand amidst screams of sheer terror from Astoria. Finally their tumbling came to a rest against a large rock. Astoria's face was distorted in fear, and there were several cuts across her cheeks and forehead. Luke scrambled on top of her and pinned her arms down above her head as sand fell from his arms and rained down on her face.

"You might think you can get loose from this hold, but just try it, and I will put my knee on your stomach," Luke informed her.

Suddenly Luke flew backward off of her and rolled to a standing position in front of her. Astoria was trying to come to terms with what had happened. One minute she was looking in the water pot, and the next minute she was flying sideways across the sand and rocks. Her face was stinging, and her leg was hurting as she struggled to sit up, but immediately after sitting up, she was plowed back over again by Luke. Astoria was suddenly on her stomach with her face buried in the hot sand while Luke slung his body across her back, pinning her down again. She kicked her legs and tried to scream, but her legs only caught empty air, and her mouth was full of sand. She began to struggle beneath Luke to free herself from this terrible attack but was not sure how to do it. Suddenly Luke's weight lifted off of her, she rolled over on her back, and began to sit up while spitting sand out of her mouth. Before she could say his name, Luke slammed into her again, and they went tumbling across the rocky sand.

"This is the way boys play, Astoria, and, when you say you give up is when I will let you go," Luke screamed in her ear, as he twisted her arm behind her back and pressed his elbows into her ribs.

Astoria screamed as Luke tugged harder on her arm, and her

anger was rising with every second that she laid there.

"Do you give up Astoria, or do you want to keep playing?" Luke asked her, as her screams subsided.

"You just better get yourself off of me right this second, Luke, before I slam this rock against your ugly face," Astoria screamed at him with every intention of doing what she had threatened.

"No, that's not the way to play the game," Luke replied to her threat. "You have to say that you give up, Astoria, or I will hold you down all day long."

"You plowed into me when I was not looking, and I do not call that fair play, Luke. Now get your nasty hands off of me, or, so help me, you are going to get your face smashed," Astoria yelled.

But to her dismay, Luke tightened his grip on her and pulled harder on her arm.

"If you are going to stand in a man's place, Astoria, you had better learn to play the game right, and do not use little girl threats to persuade me to let go until you say that you give up," he said into her ear, as she struggled against him.

"Luke! What are you doing boy?" Asher called out, as he ran across the sand to where the two children were struggling. Asher grabbed Luke by the shoulder and yanked him off of Astoria.

"Where is your mind, Luke? Have you left it hidden in the hot sand?" he yelled at him.

Astoria now had freedom to get up from the sand since Luke had been so quickly dislodged from his position. While Asher continued to scold Luke, Astoria had a chance to brush off the sand and spit it from her mouth. Her clothes were all in disarray, and her head shawl had been torn from her head while they had rolled forever in the sand. Bending down to check her leg because of the pain she felt, she rushed forward with all her might and collided against Luke, taking him down to the sand. Scrambling on top of him, she began to pummel his back with her tiny fist before Asher pulled her off of him.

I do not yet know if the lesson Luke was trying to teach Astoria was received with much gratefulness, but this I do know. She didn't want anymore to do with wrestling. After she got her self-respect back, she and Luke became closer.

****

The rest of the day was spent gathering thoughts of what I could remember of my parents' teachings to our family. It would be nice if I knew how to draw words on papyrus that I could refer to while the confrontation with Asher took place. There are a lot of reasons why I would love to learn to read and write besides times like this. There are only a few of our people who have learned this amazing work, and perhaps some day I might be fortunate enough to be taught. The children would benefit so much from this gift as well. After I have talked with Asher about the subject of desertion, I could ask him to inquire around the camps and see if there is anyone who knows how to write. Perhaps someone would be willing to teach me. If I could learn this work, then I would be able to teach my family. My thoughts are interrupted as Asher rounds the side of the tent holding the hands of Astoria on one side and Luke on the other.

Astoria's face was red and bleeding from cuts along her cheek and forehead. Her head covering was slung across her shoulder, and her clothes were dirty and rumpled. Luke was smiling as his Father deposited him on a stool before me, and Astoria stood beside her Father with her head down and her long hair hanging about her face.

"I found them wrestling behind the tent," Asher said. "I think Astoria got the worst of it, but she wanted to keep fighting even after I pulled Luke off of her. I think we had better get her cleaned up and decide what sort of punishment to give them both."

"Father," Astoria spoke up. "Please, do not blame Luke for the fight we had. It was all my fault. Luke was showing me how to wrestle because I have been pestering him to show me how to do it. We were not having a real fight, but he was showing me some different wrestling holds he knows how to do. I was yelling mainly because the sand and rocks were hot and burning my skin. Plus, I had sand in my mouth. I am sorry you thought he was hurting me, but truly he was not. So please do not punish him, but you can still punish me if that is what you decide to do." Astoria looked up at her Father's face trying to smile, but then winced from the stinging pain on her cheek.

Asher looked across at Luke sitting on the stool and asked him if what Astoria said was true.

"Astoria put up a pretty good fight, Papa, and I was real proud of her. She knows now just how to knock someone down and pin them to the ground like she did to me," Luke replied to Asher, without really answering his question.

After Luke had given his evasive answer to Asher, I busied myself getting Astoria's face cleaned up. We were going to need lots more water so both the children could have a full bath, so Asher started out with the water pots to get more water. He stopped by Mathias's tent, and I watched the two of them walking together to get the water. Asher turned his head and yelled for Luke to come along, so Luke scurried after them.

****

"I cannot abide such foolish reasoning as this," Elder Jarrod told his companion. "No matter what anyone says, whether it is Aaron or Amadeus or even my own beloved wife. I will not be moved into leaving the solid ground I stand on for the old life spent on sinking sand. I know that my God lives, and He has given a promise to bring Israel into the land He has reserved for us. He is the solid Rock of our salvation, and He is awesome in His power and might. There cannot be fashioned such a god as He. Aaron and Amadeus proposed a god fashioned by a man's hand, giving it carved eyes to see, but it cannot see. And carved ears to hear, but it cannot hear. A carved mouth to speak, but it cannot speak. The only God is the One true God who has brought us here to this place for a season. He sees all, hears all, speaks words of promise and blessing, and a future for His people."

Elder Jarrod completed his oratory, as he lifted his walking stick up and brought it down, with a sound thump on the ground. Bacchius, his companion, watched the walking stick as Elder Jarrod brought it solidly to the ground in front of his feet.

"This is surely a man who will not be moved by anyone but the true God," he thought, as Elder Jarrod drew a line across the sand with his stick. "If there is to be another leader for Israel chosen to replace Moses, the man standing before me would certainly be a good choice. It is obvious that he has walked with God for a long, long time. His great age and experiences have determined his heart toward God and His Word, and he will not allow any poisonous lies to have access to his faith."

"We have much work to do, my friend," Elder Jarrod said, as he turned and began walking toward the watering place. "There has been a report that even now Aaron is carving out a chunk of wood to fashion a false god to suit the desires for many brethren of Israel. We do not have much time to reach men who will listen, but we must give them fair warning about the disaster of this blasphemous deed."

Bacchius hurried to catch up with his friend. Walking with Jarrod made him feel important. He was not sure in which direction his desires lay concerning returning to Egypt, but when he was in Elder Jarrod's presence his heart warmed toward what the old man said.

"When I was a child, I thought as a child, but when I became grown, I put away childish things." Elder Jarrod announced, using a voice almost choked with tears. "It is not a time to play, nor is it a time to take leisure, but it is a time to work and a time to plant the good seed of God's Word. The stormy season draws near, and yet the harvest is great. The wheat and tares grow together, so we must be careful lest we be caught unaware," he said, as he picked up his walking pace.

Bacchius was not sure what Elder Jarrod said because he did not understand what it meant. But he knew that whatever it meant, it must be true because Elder Jarrod had spoken it out, and he was pleased to have the trust of the old man. His feelings of self-importance gave him cause to straighten his shoulders and puff out his chest as he walked alongside this man of God.

Elder Jarrod was striding forward like a man with a strong purpose and only a small amount of time to perform it. It took all Bacchius could do to keep up with him and walk close enough to him so others would see that he walked with Elder Jarrod. He knew in his own heart that he was only a weak man and took advantage of what others said so he could repeat it as if the wisdom came from his own mind. He also knew that he wasn't smart enough to make important decisions on his own, and his respect for the Elders of Israel was great so he trusted them with his life. Elder Jarrod was not deceived by Bacchius in anything. He knew the short comings of the younger man, but he loved his enthusiasm and spunk. Like a shepherd watching over the little lambs, Elder Jarrod had several men in his care that he looked after. He never tired of feeding these little ones with what he knew of God and His ways, and they seemed never to tire of hearing him teach either. If one has seed to sow into the fertile soil of the heart, it is a great deed done for that one who hears and receives that seed. For God's Word will not return to Him void, but it will accomplish what He sent it to do.

Jarrod saw a crowd of people near the watering place. He stood back a small distance to hear what was being talked about before joining them. Bacchius had unwittingly continued forward before noticing Elder Jarrod was not beside him. Several of the people had noticed Bacchus' approach and turned to acknowledge him. Pushing out his chest even further, he tipped his head in a slight bow toward the onlookers. He turned to one side to watch the actions of Elder Jarrod as the people greeted him. To his horror, his friend was not beside him, and he became extremely flustered because so many people were looking at him. He began to quickly look this way and that way, trying desperately to locate where his friend could be. Bacchius was almost in a panic. He began to jump in the air so he could see above the heads of the taller men as he searched for Elder Jarrod. He moved quickly between one and then another onlooker as he traced his earlier steps backward toward the edge of the crowd. His search ended when Elder Jarrod reached past another man and grasped Bacchius' arm just as he was about to pass him by. Immediately Bacchius' face gave a sign of relief in finding his friend even though he tried to pretend that everything was normal. His rapidly beating heart slowly calmed down as he mopped the sweat from his face and neck with his waist sash. The Elder gave a nod of his head in a forward direction indicating that he was listening to what some of the men were saying. All Bacchius could think about was how very glad he was that he had found his friend and that he would not be standing here all alone. He breathed a great sigh of relief and, tried to pretend, that he too, was very interested in what the other men were saying. But he continued to shoot quick glances at the elder beside him hoping he would not lose him again. What the men were talking about could not possibly be as important as this.

Chapter 13

Asher, Mathias, and Luke had recently arrived to fetch water and were standing only a few feet from Jarrod and Bacchius. They listened to the conversations of the men ahead of them. The group was talking about the events that happened earlier in the day, and there were many who demonstrated against going back to Egypt. As the conversations grew louder, Asher and Mathias spotted Elder Jarrod standing nearby. Mathias began to make his way over to Jarrod's side to have a word with him. The younger man, Bacchius, moved closer to the Elder so that no one could take his place as he watched Mathias give them a bow of courtesy.

Asher and Luke moved toward them also, and, since it was apparent that there was no room for them beside the old man, they stood just behind the three of them. Having sensed at another time that Bacchius stayed in the Elders shadow at all times, Asher quietly spoke to them his greeting and did not try to edge between them.

"We cannot stay here for a long time, my friend, and listen to the discussions," Asher told the Elder. "Mathias and I are here to fetch water so the children can have a bath. We will fill our water pots, return to our dwellings, and then we will come back here."

The old man gave a nod of his head and so the three of them continued on their way.

Asher bent down to rinse the sand from the inside of his water pot and swirled the water around inside it to cleanse any sand from it. As he did this, he could see his own reflection in a small pool of water on his left side. His thoughts began to swirl inside his mind just as the water swirled inside the pot. He remembered how staunch in faith he had been before attending the early morning meeting, and then he had been swayed by what he had heard at that meeting. His feelings were as stirred and confused about what he was to do as this water was stirred in the pot. His reflection changed as drops of water slid off the bottom of the pot and splashed into the small pool. It became more and more distorted as tiny ripples made their way across the face in the water. Almost immediately, Asher could see the lie they had fallen for and knew that his heart and mind had become as distorted as the reflection he now watched.

"Trust in the Lord with all your heart, and do not lean on your own understanding," Asher remembered that was what his Father had said to him. "Broad is the path of the wicked, but narrow is the path of the righteous. Narrow paths can be dark and mysterious and at times one cannot see beyond a deep curve in this path. That is when you must trust that God will lead you and provide safe passage. The broad path seems always to be full of snares and sliding rocks with individuals pretending to guide you safely to its end. A fool runs headlong on this path, but the wise man will wait on the Lord."

All of these wonderful sayings came flooding into his mind, and relief from the turmoil in his heart was instantly received. Mathias wondered why Asher continued to swirl the water in the pot and had not poured in a fresh supply. He shifted his weight on the other foot and loudly cleared his throat. Asher looked up at his friend and announced that his heart had just gotten right with God. Of course, Mathias asked him what had happened while he was bent over cleaning the sand from the pot. Asher sat down on a rock nearby and explained what had taken place in his heart.

"A lie can be described in such a way as making good sense, and, most of the time, it does not carry a character of harm to an individual. But there are many paths that spring off of its root and grow into a dangerous illusion. A bad or diseased tree cannot produce good fruit. Neither can a good tree produce bad fruit. In like manner, a lie is like a diseased tree that is allowed to grow alongside a good tree. It will eventually spread its sickness to the good tree. So the bad tree must be cut down and burned to ashes. A lie may sound right or look good to you, but if it is left to grow and fester, it will spread corruption and bring destruction. It must be put to death in you, or it will bring death," he told Mathias. "We are guilty of falling prey to something that sounded good and reasonable, Mathias," Asher continued, as he shifted his position on the rock, so he could stare closely into his friends' eyes. "We were on the correct path this morning, but we listened to Amadeus giving the people good reasons for going back to Egypt. We allowed that to grow and fester in our minds by giving it serious thought until we had convinced ourselves that it was the right thing to do. Do you remember the feeling of doom we experienced when we heard Aaron confirm that he would build the false god the people asked for? That was a sign from God warning us to be careful in what we heard because He had already warned us not to have any gods before him. We are not to build any likeness of things in heaven or upon this earth and attribute it to His likeness. God is creator of all the things, and we have no idea what His likeness is. It is surely not like anything we could build."

Asher finished his conversation with Mathias, rose up, and gave Mathias time to mull over what he said. He picked up the pot and filled it with water. Then he reached for the pot Mathias had. Mathias automatically extended the pot to Asher. He watched Asher fill it, but his thoughts were far away. What Asher told him caused his heart to burn. A sense of renewal and hope began taking control as tears welled in his eyes. This was truth indeed. He was grateful his friend thought enough of him to share such wonderful truth. He began feeling a sense of shame because of wavering from his staunch beliefs earlier. But he also knew that God is merciful and would not hold his weakness against him. Reaching for the full pot of water, Mathias thanked his friend for showing him the error of their ways and, especially, the truth of waiting on God for direction.

****

It had taken a long time for Asher, Mathius, and Luke to return with the water for the children's baths. Asher told me that he and Mathias were going again to the watering place and speak with Elder Jarrod. He could tell that I was not happy with him at this time. Asher leaned close as I bent over the water pot. He told me not to worry because he realized his path had been in the wrong direction earlier, and he was now on God's path. I stood up and turned toward him ready to question him thoroughly, but when I looked into his face, I could see that his eyes had a new light in them. He pulled me to him, hugged me tightly, and said we would talk about it when he returned. Naturally, the children began to giggle. At least that had not changed!

There are many different kinds of winds that blow across one's life. No one can say why this is so. But it seems that one can learn from these diverse changes, or give in, and be blown here and there with every change, like a tumble weed that has no root. We rejoice to see the different seasons of this earth come and go as God ordained. We plan our lives around the different seasons: Spring, Summer, Fall and Winter.

But when the winds of trial and tribulation come blowing through, we have no plans for our lives. How else could we learn if there were no trials to test our strength? How else would we know God's faithfulness without tribulation to help us grow and turn to Him for help? No one welcomes such fierce winds when you are the intended target for it. Times of weakness will take a foothold in your journey of life. This can be expected to happen at any time no matter how strong your faith. There is no reason for shame, but, instead, there is reason for rejoicing because your weakness is made perfect in God's strength. He is able to do far above what you could ask or think on your behalf.

My attention is quickly drawn back as the children began asking me who was going to have first turn for bathing. Since I had managed to get Astoria fairly cleaned up before the men returned with water, I told Luke he could be first to bathe. His expression was not one of joy after hearing that. He thought bathing was a big nuisance. He managed a sideways glare in Astoria's direction before stomping into the tent. Astoria watched Luke disappear inside and then announced, "I just love Luke, Mama. He has such a way with words doesn't he?"

****

Chapter 14

"We were in Egypt for over four hundred years and were forced to work under Pharaoh's cruelty for many years," Elder Jarrod was saying to the group as Asher and Mathias arrived. "Pharaoh gave orders to have our male babies killed immediately at birth. He thought Israel had multiplied too numerously and posed a dangerous threat to his nation. Our people continuously cried out to God to be delivered from this cruel Egyptian. He heard our cries and sent deliverance through Moses. Israel waited many long, hard years for this deliverance, and now we find ourselves in this wilderness as a result of God's mercy. We are not hungry, we are not thirsty, we are not sick, nor are we weary from simply gathering the food and water God provides each day. So tell me and the rest of these good men standing here, what is so difficult about waiting for God's timing to show us what He wants us to do?" Jarrod asked and spread his palm up to indicate a request for an answer. The group of men began to murmur, one man to another, nodding their heads and agreeing with Jarrod's explanation. Lifting his staff high in the air and waving his other hand for silence, Jarrod continued.

"The time Israel has spent here in this wilderness is only a water drop in a vessel compared to the centuries spent in captivity. Yet many of you say you have grown tired of waiting. Would any of you know better than God what is best for Israel? I do not think you do, since many of you have rallied to return to Egypt. So my brethren, just what will Israel be returning to? How many of you were forced to watch your sons slaughtered the very moment they came from the womb? How many of you watched your wives' eyes grow dim when joy drained from her face as the blood of your sons ran onto the floor? Our God delivered

Israel from all these terrible things and has brought us here where we stand today. If God be for us and, He surely is, then who can come against us and snatch us from His mighty hand? I will tell you the answer to that! You are the only one who can take yourself out from under God's protection and promises by your own choice, not His choice. He is in the process of raising up a nation, whose God is the Lord God Almighty. The promise of a land of our own is a true promise. The land is reserved for Israel and will belong to her forever, brethren. Do not balk and stiffen your neck against His good timing. We are finally a free people, free to worship God, free to raise our children, free to own the land He is bringing us into. Please, I beg of you. Do not turn your back on God's favor toward us. Make your knees stiff and encourage your hearts to stand with me and live beneath God's everlasting arms," Jarrod shouted, trying to raise his voice above the murmuring crowd.

Somewhere, within the density of the crowd, someone clapping his hands was heard. The men turned toward the sound, and, as they did, many others began to clap in unison. Soon, many men were clapping, shouting, and a few began to dance the old joyous dances of Israel.

****

With every whack of the chisel against the wood, Aaron vented the frustration pent up in his heart. All this was so strange and new for him, and he did not like being in the position he found himself in. He remembered the time when he joined with his brother midway Egypt and the land of Median. By request of Moses, he became a mouthpiece, speaking to Israel in Moses' stead. God would communicate with Moses, and Moses spoke to Aaron the words God wanted spoken on behalf of Israel's release. Aaron had enjoyed the position he held, and Miriam, their sister, had been instrumental in leading the women in song and praise to the Lord God.

"Where did you go, my brother, and why have you abandoned me to the whims of these people?" Aaron spoke out loud, even though there was no one to hear. "I do not have the patience and forbearance to deal with them as you have. With my own eyes, I watched you climb up that mountain as God commanded you, but, stare as I might day by day, still there is no sign of your returning. Has God abandoned you and left you upon that mountain? Is that why you do not return to Israel? Are you even now lying upon some rock with no life in your body?"

Aaron shook his head in despair.

"Or have you lost your senses and do not know the way back down? Where are the promises God gave us, and how are we to obtain them? How long before every man, woman, and child in Israel loses their life in this barren place? I was there when God opened the water, and Israel passed through on dry ground. I was there when God closed the waters upon Pharaoh's army. I was there when you spoke to the rock, and the water gushed forth before all the people. I saw all the plagues God rained upon Egypt. I watched manna form out of the morning dew each day and delighted to watch the quail fly in the camp each evening for our sustenance. I have sat here on this very stool beside you, my brother, and enjoyed many conversations as you spoke God's words to me. Almost a month has passed, and still the mountain keeps your presence hidden from me. If you are still alive, how can it be so? You have no food or water, and in the chill of the evening, where is the smoke from your fire? The people pull and tug at me from daylight until sunset, and I am weary of them all. I am not their keeper, and I have no desire to continue being their counselor. I feel like an old wine skin that's full of holes, and the strength in my body seeps out. Where is my relief if not in having the pleasure of watching you stride back into this camp? My plate overflows with the task at hand, yet my heart feels a sense of dread while I am performing it. I want to please the people and be rid of their incessant demands. I feel a sense of relief as I anticipate their departure and my release from this position I find myself in," he finished his query, as he put the finishing touches on the bull he had fashioned. "Now all that's left to do is melt the gold, plate this beast with it, and whatever shall be, shall be," he determined in his heart.

"I know we are all in a state of panic, but you, are talking as if, there is no hope left for us," Miriam announced, as she approached her brother.

****

Elder Jarrod rejoiced to see the group of men gathering in a circle, dancing, and singing the old songs of Israel. His heart warmed as many of the younger men joined in and followed the older men's dance steps. There had not been any reason for rejoicing and dancing in Egypt, and the younger men had never been taught the songs or the dances. Someone produced a flute and was playing a lively tune, keeping in sync with the dance. The group of men joined arm to shoulder with each other.

Bacchius stood aloof from the proceedings because he wasn't sure if this was a good thing or not. He watched his old friend for a sign whether this dancing would be scolded or approved. He stood ready to help either way that his friend indicated. After the rejoicing continued for some time, he assumed it must meet with Elder Jarrod's approval, or certainly he would have brought an end to it by now. The music combined with dancing caused him to tap his own toes. But becoming aware of this, Bacchius immediately restrained himself. He could see tears sliding down the Elder's face, and a smile on his lips. In like kind, Bacchius, did the same.

Soon the group ceased from their activity and started back to their separate dwellings. Each man wore a smile and was laughing, pantomiming each other's dance steps while they walked along. Elder Jarrod admonished them to keep their joy safe in their hearts, and share it with others at will.

"The joy of the Lord is our strength, brethren." he told them. "Make a joyful noise unto the Lord, praise Him in song, in the dance, and with harp and lyre for He inhabits the praises of His people."

Asher and Mathias, had joined in the dancing, also, and felt rejuvenated once again. The bleak cloud of despair could find someone else to hang over for they had entertained its malicious shadow for a while. But for us, we choose to stay under the bright rays of God's benevolence. It takes no courage to give up and fall back into the old life, but strength can be grafted onto weak vessels simply by the action of praising God.

Man's spirit is willing, but his human character is weak. His spirit and flesh are continuously at war against each other. But God has a remedy for that. Trust in the Lord with all your heart, and lean not on your own understanding. Draw close to the Lord, and He will draw close to you. The two men began to speak all of these truths to each other as they walked along, sharing them together.

Bacchius had turned and was watching the crowd as they dispersed. He wondered if Elder Jarrod would suggest that they return to their tents, for his belly desired food. There had not been time today for relaxing before a meal, and he wanted the comfort of that satisfaction met. His hopes were dejected as the old man began walking in a direction other than where their tents were.

As if reading the younger man's thoughts, the Elder told him, "Food is for the stomach, and the stomach is for food, but God will one day destroy them both. Man cannot live by bread alone, but by every word that issues forth from the mouth of God." Bacchius hoped that would not happen today for already the growling in his belly could be heard.

****

"Why do you talk into the thin air like someone who has gone mad?" Miriam asked her brother, Aaron. "You are not the only one who has reservations, about what most of the people plan to do. There has been no word from God for weeks, and the tension of the camp grows everyday. Perhaps what has been planned is the correct action to take. If it was not, then God would have surely stopped this planned return by now." Miriam watched Aaron's face for a response. "We have no communication on our own to God where we could ask His direction. Moses was the one who filled that position. Are we to continue staying here in this place until we all drop dead? My heart is also in derision over this whole affair, but my mind tells me that what I have heard about dispersing to any place we decide sounds like the thing to do. There is no future for us here in this place. How can we grow food for our families in this sand? I also desire the tasty spices we enjoyed in Egypt when we sat before the cooking pots full of tasty meat. The garlic, the fish, and the leeks were there in abundance and gave our meals a delicious, satisfying taste. We have grown tired of this manna and quail everyday."

Aaron put his chisel down on the bull he was carving and rested his hands on its back. He stared straight ahead for a time before bringing, his attention back to, Miriam.

"I sought God's wisdom when I gave advice and counseling to the people who constantly addressed my presence," Aaron breathed out with a very low whisper. "Why is it that at this crucial point in ministry I have no wisdom or courage to prevent such total blasphemy? My body is almost weakened to the point of despair, and my strength fails me when I am confronted by men who challenge anything I say. My hands continuously tremble, and the torment in my mind tears at me daily. I am not allowed any time to even morn my brother's death. Yet here I stand talking to him as though he is here. Am I not a human being with feelings and have need of counseling, also, Miriam? Who am I to have to shoulder such a despicable responsibility as building this beast which now stands before me? Why do the people come to me and appoint me to fashion a god to go before them as other nations have?" Aaron asked her all these questions, but he knew she had no answers for him.

He sat down heavily on the stool and dropped his head into his hands. Great waves of sorrow washed over his body. All he wanted to do was go to his tent and lie down for a long time of slumber and perhaps, on awakening, he would find that the last few weeks had been only a terrible dream. The sun beating down on his head made such a dream impossible to escape as he wiped the sweat from his face. Miriam brushed her hand across his sagging shoulders. Taking the water jar, she poured a cup of water for her brother.

What words of comfort could be said? She wondered. My heart breaks for him coupled with the pain of Moses' death, also.

"I can see no hope here, and to continue on with the plan at hand seems to be the best counsel I can give to you, my brother." She said, as she turned and left him to his own thoughts.

****

Astoria emerged from the tent having finished her bath, and sat down to hold Andrew for a while. She smoothed his dark hair across his head, and began chatting to the baby as though he could answer her. Andrew responded to her attention with gurgles while kicking his feet in the air. Astoria pretended the baby could understand everything she said to him and continued to talk and make funny faces at him. Luke abstractly watched the two of them for a short while before asking if he could be allowed to visit one of his friends before dinner. After cautioning him to be careful and not get dirty again, I allowed him to go.

Luke hugged my neck and gave a slight bow before rushing away. As I watched him run toward his friend's tent, I spotted Asher and Mathias coming in our direction. Asher threw his hand up to stop Luke, and the two of them stood still for a moment before Luke continued on to his destination.

As Asher and Mathias approached, I could hear them laughing. Asher came toward me with his arms outstretched while humming a tune. He took hold of my hands and began dancing, twirling about the area. Mathias and Astoria started laughing, and Astoria took the baby's hands, clapping them together to keep count with the tune Asher was humming. The look on my face must have given Asher cause to laugh as he twirled me around and around. Finally he sat me down on the stool, picked Andrew up from Astoria's lap and twirled around with him. Astoria jumped up, took the hem of Asher's robe, and the three of them giggled and twirled in a circle. Mathias, still laughing, went around the side of the tent and came back with the net and basket.

"You might consider putting an end to twirling in a circle before you get to dizzy to walk with me and gather the evening meal," he jokingly said to Asher. "It is a very good thing to have the joy of the Lord in our hearts once again," he confided, as Asher placed the baby in my arms.

"A good thing, indeed," Asher responded, "for the joy of the Lord is our strength. Make a joyful noise! Sing unto the Lord! Tell Him of your love! Dance before Him! Hallelujah!" Asher exclaimed, as he took the basket from Mathias' hand.

Then he turned to me in a deep bow, and said, "I thank you, madam, for allowing me the pleasure of dancing with you."

Laughing, I told him that he was quite welcome. They left to fetch the evening quail, and, after a short rest, I busied myself with the other preparations for the meal.

"Whatever You have done to bring this light back into my husband's eyes and heart, I am eternally grateful, dear God," I prayed, and finished the statement with several 'amen's.'

****

"The word of Truth can open blinded eyes, Bacchius," Elder Jarrod told him. "Many are the ways of the wicked, but the Lord is a strong tower of strength we can run to, my son. Do not be hasty in what you plan to do, but lay out all your plans before the Lord, and He will direct your path."

"Yes indeed," Bacchius responded.

His mind was on the hunger gnawing at his belly, and all these beautiful words did nothing to ease the pain he was experiencing. It was almost time for the quail to fly over the camp for the evening meal, and the thought of the savory meat made his stomach growl more intensely. He decided to remind his friend of this fact, but before the words left his mouth the Elder turned his direction toward their dwelling. Bacchius became so excited that he almost bypassed his old friend before he caught hold of what he was doing. Bending down and pretending to rub his foot, Bacchius allowed the old man time to get ahead of him.

"I am sort of hungry, Bacchius, since we missed our meals today," Elder Jarrod exclaimed.

Bacchius almost agreed with him too fast, but waited a few seconds.

"We did miss our meals today, I think," Bacchius commented, and waited for the old man to continue.

When nothing more was said, Bacchius heard his own stomach give a resounding growl. He quickly tried to cover it by loudly clearing his throat.

"It would not do for my friend to think that I have been waiting for this decision for quite a while," he thought.

But he still grimaced at the thought of having to catch the quails. He hoped they would not meet anyone along the way and have pause to stop and chat. At least not until he got his belly full.

Bacchius had a wife and one child that he loved dearly. His parents were still alive and occupied the tent next to his, which was across from Elder Jarrod's. Meme learned to cook from her Mother and had special things she could do to food that made it taste like heaven. She would usually gather the manna in the mornings while he slept for a while longer, but the quail was a different story. She had a fear of birds of all kinds, so he had to catch them each evening and clean them for dinner. This arrangement worked out for the both of them, but Bacchius had a lazy streak and regretted doing much work at all. He was grateful for all God had done for Israel and was looking forward to the promise just like Elder Jarrod. But having one's food come down from heaven everyday with nothing to do but collect it was not too bad a deal, he thought.

As they neared their dwellings, Elder Jarrod turned to Bacchius and wrapped his arms about the younger man's neck in an embrace of true affection.

"I will see you later, my son." he told his friend, "And may God give us grace to be quick at catching our dinner."

Bacchius nodded his head, and, after Jarrod disappeared into his tent, he rushed to his own.

Chapter 15

For days, Joshua had been aware of strange sounds coming from Israel's camp. These sounds drifted up into the heights of the mountain where he waited for Moses to return. He was very concerned and feared that something was not right, yet he knew he was to wait here, as Moses commanded him, until he returned. A soldier is faithful not to leave his post, and Joshua was in training to become a mighty soldier, though he did not know it at the time. He had always been a man of peace and tried to live according to God's word. Circumstances had placed him as the leader of Israel's make-shift military force.

The men of Israel had never encountered battle, nor had they been trained as fighting men of war, until encountering the Amalakites who secretly attacked her. Israel's men were trained for hard labor to do the will of Pharaoh in farming, in being herdsmen, in building ships, in building Pharaoh's vast city, and in all manner of labor in Egypt. Moses had commanded Joshua to gather the men of Israel and go out to fight Amaleck. In obeying that command, Israel had won victory in the battle. By praise, honor, and glory to God, the enemy fell before them.

Joshua marveled that he had eaten nothing nor drank any water, yet his body was miraculously sustained here in this high place. He had not experienced hunger or thirst for all these many days, but he did desire his leader's company. Joshua addressed Moses as "my lord" not as a slave for Moses, for indeed Joshua rejoiced in being a helper to Moses. He addressed Moses thus because he held a deep respect for this mighty man of God. It was his eager pleasure to accompany Moses and assist him in whatever was necessary. His spiritual insight was expanding greatly as he spent his days being Moses' confidant and willing participant in ministry. Joshua felt a sense of destiny in his heart, and, being a spiritual man, he attributed this feeling to God's providence.

The hour of the day had grown late with shadows stretching across the area where Joshua waited. He knew that Moses was in the presence of God further up this mountain. Enveloping Joshua was an aura of glory with light that cast a beautiful glow. It was similar to light from several candles but with breathtaking hues of color. A sense of marvelous peace and overwhelming love permeated every pore of his body. This had been with him since the first day he stayed in this place, and Moses continued up higher.

Joshua had been with the company of the seventy elders of Israel, Moses, Aaron, Nadab, and Abihu when they all ascended this mountain and saw the presence of God. When God called for Moses to come up to Him, Moses gave command for the other men to stay where they were. Then Moses and Joshua climbed higher. At a certain point, Moses told Joshua to wait there, and Moses continued ascending into the very presence of God. Joshua obeyed his leader's command and stayed where Moses left him. He wondered if the other men, who were to stay, were able to hear the worrisome sounds from Israel's encampment. They were on a lower plain than he occupied, so surely they were aware of the noises, too. He would have to wait and let God take care of it because Joshua knew he could not abandon his commanded post.

****

The group following Amadeus gathered themselves together before Aaron. They had all enjoyed a good, restful night of sleep, but Aaron had agonized over the quandary he found himself in. He was like a wild man in his thoughts, and he despised to see the break of dawn. Knowing the condition of his own heart, he realized that he resembled a man trying to drink both fresh water and salt water from the same fountain, and this cannot be. His body felt strained and weak as he rose from the mat. The work on the beast had been completed, and it sat at his workplace ready for the people to admire. Aaron's hands were sore and had numerous blisters on them from using the chisel to fashion the bull. He knew his heart was vexed, but fear of the people had driven him to complete the thing.

Aaron could hear the excited comments from the group before he emerged from his tent. They were admiring the work of a man's hands and making attempts to congratulate Aaron on the work he had done. The longer the group walked around the golden bull and talked about its beauty, the more Aaron puffed up with pride.

Soon the group began talking about making sacrifices to the bull, and Amadeus lifted both of his arms high in the air and proclaimed, "This is your god, O Israel, who brought you up from the land of Egypt."

The rest of the men began repeating the proclamation over and over again.

Aaron was afraid of them, so he built an altar before the beast and made a proclamation of his own saying, "Tomorrow is a feast to the lord."

The excited group continued rejoicing and resembled men in a state of dementia. They rushed two by two throughout the camp spreading their news about tomorrow's events to everyone. The people had emerged from their tents to gather the morning manna. News of the next days expected events spread like wildfire from one to another. The flurry of excited people became very loud as plans were made about tomorrow's celebration. The course had been set in place, and the decision had been made to sacrifice to this replication of God's glory which the people had been warned against. Now the people felt they could go anywhere they pleased since they had a visible god to go before them. Why return to Egypt? Why not continue to the promise land? After all, was not their god going before them and could be seen by any enemy who might venture to stop them? They would be like other nations now, having their own visible god to worship. And had they not seen with their own eyes his great and mighty power over these last months? This celebration had the promise of a new life and a new direction for their future, they assured each other, as they went about the preparations for tomorrow.

The ax had been laid at the root of the tree, and the Lord was the One Who held the handle in His hand. Little did the people know that God was fully aware of what had taken place, and their punishment was already on the way.

"Thou shall have no other gods before Me, neither make a graven image after My likeness and bow thyself down before it," the Lord had commanded in the hearing of all the people the day we stood before the mountain.

****

My parents told me years ago that God does not need anyone's help, but He invites our participation with Him, by our own free will. He is not a harsh task master. Neither is He blinded by His love for mankind. He is a Father who will chastise His children for their own well being. A father who does not correct his children gives notice to the world that he hates them and is not concerned for their lives. You cannot pick figs from a thorn bush. Neither can a bad tree produce good fruit. If you are without correction, then you are not His. For all of God's children will experience correction at one time or another.

When the news reached me about tomorrow's celebration, I quickly completed gathering manna and hurried back to my dwelling. Many of our friends were entertaining plans to butcher some of their cattle for the feast to go along with the different breads that could be baked from tomorrow morning's manna. There would be cheeses of all kinds, and fruit cobblers made from soaking dried fruit until plump and flavorful, and then adding honey and dumplings. Some spoke of various meat stews, and fried sweet confections. There would be fermented drinks from various dried fruits. The menu grew larger as the women compared supplies with each other. What one did not have, the other did. The children were also busy collecting patties of dried cattle dung and wood to fuel the fires needed for tonight's cooking and tomorrow, too. The men searched out their herds, tagging acceptable animals for tomorrow's sacrifices and feast. They gathered the milk and quickly took it back to their wives to use in cooking.

Many flutes were carved, cymbals were made, harps were strung, and gourds with tiny rocks inserted were brought out. Women and men practiced singing songs they remembered. The entire encampment was full of activity. The volume of frenzy rose as the day wore on, and I found it impossible to think a straight thought. Watching the activities from the front of our dwelling, Asher and Mathias stood like guards and had several occasions to turn away those who asked for this or that to help with the preparations. There were not many hands that did not have a part in the activities.

"I do not dare imagine a good night's rest for anyone tonight," Mathias said. "Israel has not been this active in quite some time. It is a sorrow that their activities are geared toward such blasphemy, and their hearts and minds have been darkened by such as this. The pillar of cloud by day and the pillar of fire by night perform their intended duties that God sent them to perform, yet Israel has become blinded by their own desires, and pays no attention to the wonder of it all. I, also, was blind, but when the Light came, I was given sight."

Mathias wiped a tear from his eye.

Asher had been plaiting a rope from goat hair while he sat in front of our tent. He completed the rope and gave it a sound tug to test its strength before standing and winding it to one of the tent poles.

Asher commented as he inspected the woven rope.

"I think this rope is a good, strong work of strength. It reminds me that God is in control of His earth, and His strength can be tested by His great love and design. Everything that is here was designed and created by Him, and there is nothing either here on this earth, or in Heaven above which He did not create. You and I are able to make certain things for our work or for pleasure, but we cannot make them without using something that God has created already. We are limited, but He is without limits. We are weak, but He is strong. We praise God for His goodness, and He inhabits the praises of His people. Our thoughts are not His thoughts because His thoughts are far above what we could ask or think."

"I wonder how tomorrow will turn out, the plans and such I mean," Mathias said. "Are you attending the festivities Asher? Perhaps in hopes of snatching some of the people from the fire of their demented actions?"

Asher kept his attention on the rope.

"I have considered it myself but have not made my decision." Mathias continued, placing his hand on Asher's shoulder and turning him around to face him. "I know the agony in your heart over what is happening. I have the same agony in mine. The tears in your eyes give your hidden pain a voice that cannot be silenced, either by hiding your face or by doing nothing," Mathias stated and patted his friends shoulder.

"Mathias," Asher growled, "we have done all the good that can be done. We have walked this encampment from end to end and tried to reason with our brethren but to no avail. Have we managed to turn just one from his wicked ways?"

"Perhaps not," Mathias replied, "but all it takes for evil to grow is for good men to do nothing. If we do not give all we have left in doing the right thing then we should be ashamed to call ourselves satisfied. There still may be one that will listen, but, unless the workers are in the field, the harvest cannot be reaped."

"What you said cuts to the very marrow of my bones, old friend," Asher admitted. He brushed past Mathias and returned to his stool.

Mathias gave Asher a moment to reflect, and then Mathias began speaking again.

"The word of God is sharper than a two-edged sword, Asher. It divides between the flesh and the marrow and between the thoughts and intents of the heart. It shines a light into our hearts so we can see our faulty ways. A light so bright that you cannot ignore its shining. It is another work of God's grace to help us achieve good character and to straighten our crooked paths," Mathias replied.

Asher knew from listening to his friend, coupled with his own beliefs, that Mathias was right. This was not a time to throw one's hands into the air and give up, but it was a time for the shaking of grain and separating the chaff. "Plaiting a rope of goat hair could get you into some tight places in your thinking."

Asher mused. "But admiring God's word is far better for one's eyes to behold than all the works of a man's hands, any day."

****

I sat inside the tent listening to the growing noise outside. The excited voices of men, women and children, as they scurried back and forth, sent waves of fear lapping against my heart. Baby Andrew had finished nursing, so I picked up the precious bundle and laid him across my knees, gently patting his back.

"He is such a happy baby," I thought, as I watched him squirming about on his belly. 'How nice and calm life would be if we all could keep the innocence of babies in our hearts. But instead there is a flow of self-satisfying will, which seeks opportunity at every turn to get what it wants."

"Be as wise as serpents but as harmless as doves."

This was a true quote Mama had taught me. But to know how to perform such a glorious thing in ones life seemed to always be just out of reach.

"If there is to be good in the world, then good seed must be planted, watered, and tended," Mama had instructed her children. "The beauty of the flower is only the visible result of the difficult, unseen stages of growth the plant must experience before the end result can be enjoyed. In the center of this beautiful flower there are seeds that have the exact likeness of its kind. The seeds have all the potential to produce more plants with beautiful flowers if they are collected and planted and tended to properly. In like manner, God gave us beautiful children. He is expecting us to plant His words in them, watering them by washing His word over them often, and tending them by pulling away weeds of selfishness, laziness and unkindness which can choke the life of God's

Word in them. As those children grow through different stages of life, they have the potential to produce a beautiful Godly character with all the good seed residing in their hearts to continue the cycle with their own children." Mama had explained this to us on a day when we helped her with her beautiful potted flowers, which she had setting all around the front of our home.

I placed Andrew on the mat to change his diaper. My memories of Mama and some of her teachings had managed to drown most of the outside noise. I could faintly hear the low murmur of Asher and Mathias' conversation just beyond the tent door. After finishing with Andrew, I turned him on his belly and allowed him time to kick and gurgle until he grew quiet and laid his little head down to sleep. Ever so quietly, I slipped away to ask Asher the whereabouts of Luke and Astoria. Asher pointed to a small corner behind Mathias where he had placed a mat. Both children were fast asleep. Luke's arm was lying across Astoria's stomach. Mathias looked up at me and smiled as I passed in front of his stool to hang the wet diaper to dry.

"It is necessary to fetch more water, husband." I said to Asher, "Andrew's diapers need to be washed, and we will need water for cooking tonight. I would enjoy a chance to go for a walk about the camp later today if you would be willing to come with me." He and Mathias rose at the same time to go fetch the water.

Asher looked at me and nodded his head, and I saw his eyes were wet with tears.

"Is everything going to be alright in Israel, Asher?" I asked, as he bent low and brushed his lips across my forehead.

****

It was a beautiful evening for a long stroll around the different camps, but I knew that my husband was leery about straying too far from home. We had met and spoken with several acquaintances along our way. Just to watch what was going on all around us was very interesting indeed. The children were calling out greetings to their friends, and everything seemed to be almost perfect, but the entire encampment was on the brink of learning a very severe lesson.

Mathias insisted he stay and watch Andrew so we as a family could walk and have time together. His weathered, joyous face belied the worry in his heart as he shooed us away in his old bearish manner. Our stroll continued on past Elder Jarrod's tent, and we waved at the old man and, of course, Bacchius, too. I saw Bacchius look quickly toward the Elder's face before responding back at us with a wave.

Suddenly I heard my name called. Turning toward the sound, I saw Jillian motioning us to come over to where she was helping prepare delicacies for tomorrow's big feast. Luke and Astoria ran over to the area where Jillian stood, and I saw her give the children something from her hand. Jillian watched our approach and laughed as the children quickly finished the treat she had given them.

"That was very kind of you to give them a treat, Jillian," I said to her while bending down to wipe the smear of honey from Luke's cheek. "It has been a while since they had sweet goodies except for the few berries we are able to find at times."

Jillian smiled and assured me that watching the children eat the cookie so quickly had given her all the thanks she needed. Wiping her fingers on a towel, Jillian asked me about what food I planned to prepare for tomorrow. Feeling Asher's fingers tighten against mine, I simply shrugged my shoulders as a sign that I did not know.

"Well whatever you bring, I am sure it will taste wonderful," she answered, as she turned her chin to one side and peered at me as if she had another question to ask.

I quickly avoided her next question by suggesting that we had best be getting back to see about Andrew.

"Thank you, again Jillian for the cookies," I told her, "and I am sure we will be just fine with whatever I decide to prepare."

As we turned to leave, she asked if we would please stop by her tent on the way home and tell her husband that she would be there soon. Asher and I both nodded, and each of us took a child's hand and started off.

"Why oh why, dear Lord of Glory, must it be this way? The people of Israel have good solid hearts and are people of family blood. They have stiffness about them in ways, but that stems from so many years of having to live in mistrust of others. Now that we are a free people, it is hard to release all we have endured throughout our generations in just a few months of time. The great promise You gave to Abraham has been a thorn in the sides of many of our people. They have had to endure terrible treatment for so many harsh cruel years that the promise seemed to be some fable we all lost hope of ever realizing. Dear God, have mercy on us all, I pray, and do not cast us entirely away from Your mighty plans for Israel."

My mind began another trip back to teachings my mother gave me.

"Listen! For I say that when you set your hand to doing a work, then do the work with all your heart and not like it is of small consequence. You never know who might examine your work, and, if it has been done well, you will receive the praise due to you. Perhaps God will be the One who will examine your work and your motive that drove you to begin the work in the first place. Possibly, you think that your voice will only be heard in the ears of the listeners that cross your life, but think about the words that have been passed from one generation to another. Are you able to live for centuries and speak to every person who walks on this earth? Certainly not! But your words and your works can outlive you for as long as God pleases to keep them preserved for generations to come. Do not be blinded in your vision like when you walk into a tunnel and can only see a small ray of light coaxing you toward the end. Shake yourself loose from the fetters that bind your vision. When you walk into an open plain, you are able to look straight ahead of you, yet your eyes see everything that is all around. Be aware that you are not alone no matter if the silence you hear is roaring in your ears. God is everywhere and can be called on from any place, at any time, and will answer your deepest heart's cry no matter who you are. If you lack wisdom for your life, you may ask God for wisdom, and He will supply you with it if you ask with an open and honest heart without doubting. A person's life is like a vapor of smoke. It is here one day and can be gone the next. Do good to all people when it is in your power to do so, and owe no one anything but the courtesy due another human being. Do not rush to judgment against another, but give place for a fair hearing to determine if the charge has any merit. Remember when you point the finger at another person, there are four fingers on your hand that point back at you. Be wise and do not entangle yourself, or your property, or your livelihood in another person's debt. Perhaps you think by signing your permission to be a guarantee for another person's debt will turn out to be a good thing. But no one can know what lies in the future, and you could be called to pay the debt in full. You will surely lose your savings and possibly be thrown into the debtor's prison. If your neighbor is in need of something to eat or perhaps good counseling, and he comes to your door in the middle of the night asking you for such, even though you are inconvenienced at this hour, you will arise and give him what he needs. A piece of bread or a kind word in due season will possibly be the light he needs to give him hope."

Mama was a very wise woman.

"Oh, if only I knew how to write. I could put all of these good teachings from my parents on papyrus and save them to share with the whole world," I mused while we walked toward our dwelling.

The delicious aroma of different delicacies being prepared filled the afternoon air in the camps. The time was drawing near for the quail to fly into the camps so we quickened our step to get back. The people were visiting with one another, and there was lots of laughter and conversation everywhere. Luke and Astoria were dragging their feet in hopes of being invited for another treat. We stopped by Jillian's tent as we promised to do and informed her husband that she would be along soon. Asher decided he would stay and talk a while and said we could continue on home.

Mathias was sitting in front holding Andrew as we arrived. Andrew was enjoying the sound of the old man's voice and his little chuckles could be plainly heard. I relieved Mathias of the baby and thanked him for taking care of him. His twinkling eyes told me that the child had been no trouble to him. He landed a smacking kiss on Andrew's cheek before giving him to me.

"You can find Asher across the way at Jillian's tent," I told Mathias. "He wanted to visit for a bit. The delicious smells around here are making me hungry, so maybe the quail will be a little early today," I remarked as he made his way around the tent to fetch the net and basket.

"I have hoped for that very thing, Leeanna," Mathias responded as he tousled Luke's hair and invited him to come along with him.

I nodded my head toward Luke, and the two of them started across the way toward Jillian's tent.

I began washing the baby's diapers and strung them out to dry. After that, I started making preparations for dinner. I could see several men making their way out to catch quail, and the noise began dieing down during this time. The bustle going on around the camps put me in memory of our wedding day feast. I guess in a way tomorrow's events would be a kind of wedding with different ones sacrificing before an altar and a big feast afterward. But to what were they promising their allegiance? And how could a carved idol do anything good or bad for anyone? The people are only ignorant about what they propose to do. These are good and decent people who are trying to do what they think is right. It makes no difference what one thinks is right. It still can be deadly wrong. My feeble answer to Jillian's question was an excuse to escape without saying what I really thought about tomorrow's plans. I will remedy that mistake when I get a chance tomorrow. Maybe she will listen to me. I know she is a believer in God, but she needs some light of truth to shine in her heart and mind.

When we settled down to rest that night, the noise had surprisingly quieted down. I suppose the people were all tired and wanted to have a good night's rest from their many activities.

Chapter 16

The new day broke with a beautiful sunrise stretching gorgeous rays of color across the eastern sky like layers of colored, shimmering silk. I caught my breath and became lost in the beauty unfolding before me as I enjoyed each glorious birth of a new and beautiful color. It looked like God was putting out His glorious display across the heavens to show mankind the truth of His works and existence. There is not a corner of this earth that God's glory has not shown great signs of His existence. God is not a man that He should make a lie. There is no excuse for anyone to claim that He does not exist.

The rainbow we see that graces the arc of the sky after a rain is God demonstrating to man that He still and always will uphold His promise to never destroy the earth by water again. Though this earth belongs to God, and He may do with it as He pleases, His love for mankind is mighty, and their death does not bring Him joy.

Everyone will experience death at some time. So to die and be translated in spirit from this earth to heaven requires a spiritual agreement signed with God's blood between the two parties, and He will give this gift of eternal life to each one who seeks His unlimited mercy.

Man's spirit will live forever either with God in heaven or banished from God's presence. The choice is up to each individual person. God has no grandchildren. Each person, whether you are a man, woman or child, must willingly accept God as your salvation with your entire heart, and only then are you called His child. God is an ever-living, vibrant Spirit Who is without genealogy. He has always existed and always will. He is all wise, all merciful, all caring, all power, all seeing, and pure love. Not one bird can fall to the ground without His knowledge of it. He knows the count of hairs on your head. There is nothing you have ever done that He does not know about. He hears the faintest whisper and is able to answer before it even leaves your heart. Like your human father, God will not give everything you desire, and this is for your own good.

My thoughts and commune with God are interrupted as Asher stepped out of the tent to join me. Taking my outstretched hand, he gently sat down beside me as his eyes took in the beauty of the sunrise. The gentle breeze that swayed the strands of his hair was scented with the smell of lilies in full bloom. This moment gave us pause to be an audience with eager anticipation to watch God design every wisp of beautiful color across the stage of His sky. Soon this moment would be left behind in our memories, but there were more beautiful dawns to come.

This day having started so lovely would end in much tragedy. No one could have known what this day's events would mean for Israel. The people would sit down to eat and drink and rise up to play and quarrel. All too soon, the rest of the tragic day began to unfold.

****

The rush of activity was not long in coming within the camps of Israel. Upon returning from milking and watering our herd, Asher and Mathias reported that many men were taking the cattle each had tagged the day before and gathering before the golden bull. The women and children were still gathering manna and were to bake more food for the feast. Astoria and Luke had quickly gathered the manna for our table and was busy grinding it into flour. After finishing nursing, bathing, and changing the baby, I began preparing our meal.

****

Aaron stood watching the gathering crowd as they brought animals to be sacrificed before the golden bull fashioned at their request. He knew this was wrong but felt helpless to do anything to prevent such madness. There had been no man to stand beside him each day as he bantered with the people over returning to Egypt. There was a small group of men who stood on the outer fringes of the crowds and tried to assuage such a regrettable plan as this. But their voices failed to penetrate the hard headed mob just as his voice had failed to do. Now the day was upon them, and Aaron had foolishly proclaimed this day to be "a day unto the lord." The people were no longer displeased with their position in this wilderness. They had dispersed from before the bull yesterday with high hopes and great plans to have a feast. The officiator of the enlarging crowd was Amadeus, and he claimed a high seat beside the lofted bull so he could be seen by everyone.

Amadeus began to issue commands to the people on how each planned event would be carried out throughout the day. Aaron stood to one side and listened as various reasons were given for each expected sacrifice. Amadeus gave a command to build huge fires to roast the meat after each animal was sacrificed and butchered. The people could almost taste the delicious meat as they imagined the huge spits with various meats being turned and roasted above the heaped coals. There were so many who were willingly led into this despicable charade. The people were only concerned with themselves, the day's events, and tomorrow would take care of itself.

Some began building the huge fires Amadeus called for, and some began setting up a place for the food and drink everyone would be sharing. The flutes were being played as families began arriving with their contributions of food. Amadeus commanded all the people present, to partake in the sacrifices, and then the feast afterward. No food was to be uncovered or eaten until everything was properly completed as he instructed. Everyone must stand together and be of one mind, one voice, and one heart on this great day. The people had gathered their daily portion of manna as normal, but no one had eaten anything. All food would be brought to the feast and shared.

****

"Are you finished cooking for the feast? The people are beginning to gather even now." Jillian called out as she approached where I stood preparing our morning meal.

My mind had been occupied on getting our meal ready, and her voice startled me. Looking up, I saw that Jillian carried a basket laden with food in her arms. I placed the last hoecake on the platter and removed the pan from the fire before rising to my feet to answer her question.

"No Jillian," I began. "My family will not be attending the day's activities. What is taking place in the appointed area beyond us is not right, and we will have no part in it."

I watched her face for a reaction and was not surprised to see shock appear on it.

Setting her basket down, she looked at me wide-eyed with wonder as she responded to my statement.

"What do you mean by saying it is not right? Leeanna, are you not aware that most all Israel are attending the celebration today? Aaron has fashioned for us a fine golden representation of God's strength and might so we can look on him, sacrifice to him, and serve him as he desires. What is not right about that, Leeanna?"

"That is not a representation of our God, Jillian." I said. "That is an idol. It is a mere chunk of wood carved and fashioned by a man's hands. It cannot and will not ever represent the God we are to serve. Remember the day Israel gathered before the mountain, and God spoke to us with His own voice, Jillian? What was the very first command He spoke to us? Tell me if you will?"

I saw her shrink back, and her eyes grew cloudy trying to recall what had been said.

"You shall have no other gods before Me," was her whispered reply.

"Go on and finish the rest of it, dear," I encouraged her.

Jillian continued, "And you shall not make any image in My likeness nor the likeness of anything either here on this earth nor in the heavens above and bow yourself down to it."

She looked at me through tears, and her lips trembled as she responded to what her own mouth had spoken.

"Oh my, what have I done? How could I have been so blind? How could all of us have been so blind? We thought we were doing what God would be pleased with, but, instead, we have done a very horrible thing and attributed His glory to a golden beast."

Jillian sank down on her knees moaning and rocking back and forth, as tears of repentance washed over her face and heart. I allowed her to stay in her position for a while so she would begin to remember more of what God had said to us. The ugly veil had been pulled aside from her heart, and now the truth had access to reclaim its place there. God is a merciful God, and He delights to open our eyes if we are willing to hear with our ears and receive with our hearts. If we will turn and repent of our wrongs, He is quick to cleanse us from all unrighteousness. After a few moments, I put my arm around her shoulders and assisted her in standing.

"There are others we have to reach, Jillian, and we have only a short time to do it," I said.

I was relieved that she agreed to go with me to seek them out.

People were rushing back and forth in all directions as Jillian and I made our way toward the center of the activities. After giving the children their food, I left Astoria in charge of watching Andrew and Luke until I returned. Asher and Mathias were campaigning to turn others from this blasphemous deed. Asher did not know I intended to campaign on my own. He instructed the children and me to stay home.

On approaching the area where the people merged, Jillian and I began to speak quietly with many women present, working our way through the crowd. There were a few who finally listened but were afraid of what their husbands would do. We managed to convince a few to help us mingle through most of the crowd and told them to pretend that they were visiting certain friends. As Jillian and I approached the front of the group gathered around the dreaded golden idol, I tried not to look at the despicable thing. But I could not prevent my eyes from seeing all the blood running down the altar before it. The last of the animals tied there were making frightened noises. The stink of blood filled the air. Amadeus and several of his assistants were before the altar with long, sharp knives collected from the battle with Amalek. Another group was butchering each animal in turn after it had been bled upon the dastardly altar.

My stomach began to heave like I was about to vomit, but I continued on with the necessary mission and tried to look no more at the gory scene. The men cut the animals throats and continued to shout praises to this god as they dashed the animals head against a large rock to assure its death. Suddenly, someone grabbed my arm and began pulling me into the cheering crowd. I automatically began to fight and resist, but whoever it was had strong hands. Jillian had been right behind me, and I could hear her angry screams as if she was fighting someone off, too. There was such noise all around me. People were shouting and jeering so loud I felt no one would hear our screams or even try to rescue us.

"Well, look at this!" I heard a male voice growl in my ear, "It is the pretty little thing I had the misfortune to run into a few days ago," he sneered. "She does not have her body guard lurking around her this time, does she? There is a fine place over behind those rocks where we can go and get to know each other real good." He began pulling me along with him. Some of the men standing near to us did not know what was being done to me. They laughed and winked their eye at the stranger as if they thought he was dragging his wife along. I tried to call out for their help, but this only caused them to laugh harder, and they turned back to watch the display taking place at the altar. Thoughts for Jillian's safety rushed across my mind as I screamed out her name. My arm felt as though it was being wrenched from its socket because of his strength. My heart was pounding, and the noise of the crowd around me drowned out all my attempts at screaming for someone to help me. I was being helplessly dragged by my arm through the crowd of men, women, and children. My head was spinning because of the pain in my arm, and the faces I saw passing my sight began to have a hideous contortion to them. I remember stumbling, and something hard and sharp punctured my leg as I fell forward into the dust being stirred up by so many feet.

The next thing I remember, I am lying in a large meadow of long, tall grasses all around me. And there is a sound of trickling water from somewhere that I cannot see. It is cool here, and the birds are singing.

"Have I died and gone to heaven?" I wondered, "What about my baby and the other two children. Where were they in this calm, peaceful place? I hear my husband's voice as he keeps calling me over and over again. Why must I go from my blissful rest so soon and answer his insistent call? Will he please allow me a few more precious moments in this sanctuary?"

From somewhere in the distance a woman was screaming the name of Jillian.

"Where can Jillian be?" I wondered, "Would someone please help that woman find Jillian? Asher, would you please help find Jillian so I can lie here in this wonderful place for a while longer? Oh, why does he keep calling me? Why is there no one to help the poor woman who keeps screaming? I may as well get up and help her for it is evident that no one else is going to."

I try to get up but my legs and arms are too heavy for me to move.

"Someone must be holding me down, someone that I cannot see."

I felt water run across my lips, and I began slipping my tongue through my lips to have a taste of it. I felt a sharp pain in my arm as I tried to reach for the source of the water and gasping from the pain caused me to cough. Fighting the waves of pain in my arm, I tried to move my legs again so I could stand up, but another pain shot through my leg.

"My God," I prayed, as I lay there in the grass, "will you help that woman find Jillian and help me get up? And will you please tell my husband to stop calling my name?"

"You have rested for a while in the embrace of your God, Leeanna. Now it is time for you to awake and continue your life. I have many plans for you and your loved ones, and there is much need for your teaching concerning My little ones. Your family is in great concern for your health, but you will recover quickly. Awake now child and be restored to your loved ones," a beautiful Voice said to me.

Opening my eyes caused the woman's screams to stop. Asher was lying beside me calling my name with great sobs.

"Why do you keep calling me when you can see I am here beside you, Asher?" I whispered to him.

The sun was bright in my eyes and I saw the sky with a few clouds above me.

"Why are you bleeding Asher? Are you injured?" I tried to reach my hand toward my husband.

My arm would not do what I wanted. Instead of touching his face, my hand flopped across his shoulder.

"Leeanna!" Asher said, raising his head from the sand. "You are still with me!" He tried to rise up on his elbow.

"Why are we lying about in the sand, Asher?" I asked him.

He dropped his head toward the sand and began to cry again.

"Husband, what is the matter with you, and tell me why are you bleeding?"

There was no answer and alarm caused me to scream his name. "Asher!"

"He will be fine, Leeanna." I heard someone tell me, "He is merely resting for a moment. We will take care of him."

Turning my head in the direction of the voice, my eyes began to focus on Mathias standing above me.

"Mathias?" I asked.

"Yes, Leeanna, it is me. There was a fight between Asher and the man who was dragging you away. Asher had seen you before the man grabbed you, but he could not reach you. We were headed in your direction, but you were moving in and out of the crowd so quickly he did not have time to reach you. Asher fell and hit his head on a rock when he was fighting that man. That's why he is bleeding. Elder Jarrod and his group are holding the man who attacked you. I do not think you have to worry about him anymore, Leeanna. After they finish with him, I believe he will think long and hard about trying to molest a daughter of Israel again. You know that some among us are not of our people, and he is one of those," Mathias informed me.

Some men came and helped Asher standup and walk. Asher smiled weakly at me and tried to reach down to carry me. Mathias quickly scooped me up into his arms, and we started heading toward home.

"O my dear Lord!" I said, "Jillian! Where is Jillian?"

Mathias informed me that she was just fine. The man who had grabbed her arm, pulling her into the crowd was her husband. He meant her no harm. He had seen her pass before him, tried to call out to her, but she could not hear him. So he reached past a man, grabbed her arm, and pulled her into the crowd. She was screaming for a few minutes before she realized who he was, but now she is fine.

The noise other people made, whooping and hollering was deafening. Mathias had to return the cup he used to bring water for me. He stopped where everyone was gathered to feast. Asher used one of the pitchers setting on a table to wash his face with water. The cool water refreshed him, and he offered to carry me in Mathias' stead.

"There is no need for anyone to carry me like I am a bushel of flour," I responded. "Set me down on my feet, Mathias, I want to try to walk if it is possible."

Mathias and Asher began protesting, but finally Mathias did as I asked.

"She is a very headstrong woman, Asher, as we are both learning," Mathias said.

There were stations set up for the different roasted meats and other food. The food was covered with long cloths and held down at the sides with rocks to keep sand from blowing into the food as the sacrifices were taking place. Everyone had gathered in a great mob to eat because no one had eaten any food by command of Amadeus. Being the self-appointed officiator of these festivities, he stood with his hands held high in the air and invoked everyone to silence. He began walking to and fro, holding his hands low over the covered food before him. He was loudly asking blessings on what all the people had accomplished this today.

When he completed his oratory, Amadeus shouted, "And now let the results of our labors be revealed, eaten, and enjoyed in the sight of our god," he pointed toward the golden bull.

The entire crowd erupted in shouts, waving their hands furiously above their heads. The women sprang forward lifting the covers off the food as the men rubbed their hands together in anticipation of the great spread before their eyes. The women jumped back horrified at what they saw. The entire spread of food which they worked so faithful on preparing had become a writhing mass of worms.

"What is the meaning of this," some of them cried out loudly. "How could such a thing be? We prepared good food, and now the entire spread is full of worms!"

They desperately slapped and swatted with cloths, trying to fling the worms to the ground, but there was too many. The men started shouting at their wives, questioning their cooking. Did you use bad flour? Why do you embarrass us this way? The women frantically searched to find any food that did not have worms, so the feast would not be a total loss. But there was nothing edible to be found, except the meat which had been sacrificed. Everyone rushed to take a portion of meat for themselves, and soon there wasn't enough for the number of people present. The people began quarreling with each other. Fights broke out all over the area. Some fought right in the midst of the wormy food.

Mathias scooped me up in his arms again and yelled over his shoulder to Asher,

"We had best get away from this immediately."

Nodding his head in the direction of our tents, we fled from the area as fast as we could go. We did not stop until we reached the safety of our tent.

Upon arrival, the children came running out to greet us, and Jillian emerged from our tent directly behind them. She explained that she came here to sit with the children after Mathias told her they found me. My children's faces never looked more beautiful to me. My heart is ever grateful to God Almighty for saving Asher and I so we could return home to our family. Jillian left in a while, promising to check on us later.

Chapter 17

And the Lord said to Moses, "Go down from here for your people whom you have brought out of the land of Egypt have corrupted themselves. They have turned aside quickly from the way which I commanded them; they have made for themselves a molten calf and have worshipped it and have sacrificed to it. They have said, "This is your god, O Israel, who has brought you out of the land of Egypt." And the Lord said to Moses, "I have seen this people, and, behold they are a stiff-necked people; now therefore let Me alone, that my wrath may be kindled against them, and that I may destroy them and I will make of you a great nation."

But Moses prayed before the Lord his God and said, "Not so, O Lord, do not let Your wrath kindle against Your people whom You have brought forth out of the land of Egypt with great power and with a mighty hand. Why should the Egyptians say, "It was for their injury He brought them out to slay them in the mountains and to consume them from the face of the earth? Rest from Your fierce anger and be reconciled concerning the evil deed of Your people. Remember Abraham, Isaac, and Jacob, Your servants, to whom You swore by Your own self and You did say to them, "I will multiply your descendants, as the stars in the heaven, and all the land that I have spoken of I will give to your descendants, and they will inherit it forever."

"And the Lord was reconciled concerning the evil which He had purposed to do to His people." (EX: 32:7-14)

Moses turned and went down from the mountain, and the two stone tablets of the testimony were in his hand. The tablets were written on both sides. The tablets were the work of God, and the writing was the writing of God engraved upon the tablets.

****

When Joshua heard the noise of the people fighting, he said to Moses when he approached, "There is a noise of war in the camp."

Moses said to him, "It is not the sound of the cry of mighty men. Neither is it the sound of the cry of weak men, but it is the sound of sin that I hear."

And as soon as Moses and Joshua came near to the camp, Moses saw the calf and the cymbals. Moses' anger raged. He threw the tablets out of his hand and broke them at the foot of the mountain. He took the calf which they had made, burned it in the fire, and filed it with a file until it was ground into dust. And he scattered the dust upon the water, and made Israel drink of it.

And Moses said to Aaron, "What has this people done to you that you have brought so great a sin upon them?" (EX: 32:15-21)

Aaron said, "Do not let your anger rage. You yourself know these people that they are bad. For they said to me, "Make us gods to go before us, as for Moses who brought us up out of the land of Egypt, we do not know what has become of him."

And I said to them, "Whosoever has any gold bring it to me. So they brought it to me. Then I cast it into the fire, and it became this calf."

When Moses saw that the people had sinned (for Aaron had caused them to sin and to leave a bad name behind them) Moses stood in the gate of the camp and said, "Who is on the Lord's side? Let him come to me."

All the Levites (descendants of Levi, one of the twelve sons' of Jacob) gathered themselves together to Moses.

And Moses said to them, "Thus says the Lord God of Israel. Every man put your sword by your side, and go in and out from door to door throughout the camp, and slay every man, his brother, his friend, and his neighbor."

The Levites did according to the word of Moses, and the people that fell that day were about three thousand men.

Moses said to them, "Strengthen yourselves today before the Lord, every man with his son and with his brother, for a blessing shall come upon you today." (EX: 33: 22-29)

The terror heard and felt throughout the camps of Israel that day cannot be described. It was a day when God's wrath tempered with mercy and justice brought a time of chastisement to His people, Israel.

God is not a man that He should lie. Neither a son of man that He should repent.

There were so many that fell by the sword that day. All the preaching and teaching about the sin of disobedience in worshipping and bowing before false gods had done very little. We had been able to snatch only a few from making that terrible mistake. The Lord our God had shown great mercy in His anger, and the people who were spared that day surely realized it.

There will come another day of God's wrath, Elder Jarrod told us, a day of troubling and gnashing of teeth when God will bring an end to this earth and mankind. But in His great mercy and love, He will preserve those who have come to Him and believed on Him for their salvation. These will live through eternity with Him as the sons and daughters of Almighty God, kings and priests before the Lord God our Redeemer forever.

If there was ever a person who had a zeal for God, that person would have to be Moses. He had been up on Mt. Horeb, in God's presence, for forty days being taught and groomed in the Word of God. His ambition took its root in God on the day he was called, and given God's promise that He would never leave him nor forsake him, but would be to him a tower of strength. Moses communed with God face to face. Moses' heart for his people is to see them established in the Promised Land, and become a great nation under one God, the Lord God Almighty. The time he spent with God on Mt. Horeb, was a time of teaching, and learning, and a time of getting to know God, in all His magnificent ways. God talked to Moses concerning His plans for, Israel, with all the ordinances, and principles, to establish a people of worship, and high calling. God wrote all those things down on the stone tablets with His own writing. He knew the people would need to be rehearsed in these things over and over again. It was crucial that Moses understand God's intent concerning the rituals of worship, and why they must be done in a certain fashion. God is Holy, and those who would worship Him must do so with holy hearts. The principles written down on the tablets would lead the people into how to achieve holiness. These same tablets of divine instructions were the tablets which Moses cast down and broke in the sight of all Israel.

One can understand that even before these instructions were handed down many of them had been totally broken, starting with disbelief and ending in tragedy. When Moses threw the tablets and broke them, he unknowingly demonstrated that all people everywhere, had in some ways, broken God's law. It would take a sinless Savior as a go between, not to repair the broken laws, but to fulfill them before God.

This Savior, who was to come, would take into His own body all the sins of mankind, and with the sacrifice of His life's blood, would bring redemption and reconciliation, between God and mankind. This Savoir, Who would be broken on a cross would not bring a curtain of tragedy on people, but would bring them victory because of His obedience to God.

The people looked on Moses as their savior from the tragic life of slavery, and indeed Moses was a "type" of the Savior to come. God would take upon Himself a body of flesh and blood, just as mankind had, but without the sin mankind carries. He would become the self-appointed sacrifice in order to bring the people total salvation. These precious truths that would one day come into being, were in the heart of God from before the very foundations of the earth's creation.

Moses, having been in close communion with God, had a premonition of things which were to come, but his work now was to assist God to groom and grow a nation of holy people. Holy not by themselves, but holy because of Who God is and their obedience to Him.

****

The new day broke upon a camp filled with silence except for mournful sounds which erupted from families who had lost their loved ones by the swords of the Levites the day before. As the morning dew began to melt on the ground, the manna appeared for our food just as it always had since the first day God sent it. The people quietly slipped out from their tents and collected the manna but without the chattering and laughing. It seemed as if a dark blanket had come upon the camps during the night and lingered into the light of day. The people quickly gathered their portion and went directly back to their tents. No one lingered behind to chat or gossip with their neighbors but kept to themselves in fear concerning their participation in worshiping the golden bull.

My family had been spared the edge of the sword as many others were spared also. We had faced the Levite who came to our dwelling. His sword dripped with the blood of the dissenters. He stood before us looking closely at our family. Then as if he had heard a certain instruction, he simply turned and walked away. Asher, Mathias, and I broke into praises to God for sparing our family this tragic punishment and destruction.

We were concerned for our neighbors. Our hearts and prayers were fervently begging for mercy for them. It is a true saying that the effectual fervent prayer of a righteous man or woman avails much. A person cannot go wrong by spreading their hopes, fears, sorrows, pleading, and plans before the Lord. He hears our prayers, and He is able to divide between what is of the heart and what is of one's own selfish desires. God delights to give His people the desires of their hearts if those desires are within His perfect will and accomplishes works which are for the good and well-being of others.

He is not stingy with His gifts. Neither is He foolish or can be fooled. He is able to see past the emotions one stirs up in hopes to turn His hand. He looks directly at the true situation. He makes judgment within His own wisdom and gives according to the true need. Whether that is to adjust your thoughts in line with His or for the true need you asked for without selfish desire.

****

Asher and Mathias slipped out to walk the camps trying to bring some means of comfort to the hurting people. You must never go to one who is hurting or was hurt by the very thing you had warned them against and proudly puff yourself up saying, "I told you so, or I warned you about that, or see what has happened because you would not listen to me?" That is not a time to heap accolades and praises on your own shoulders, but it is a time for crying with those who cry, mourning with those who mourn, or praying with and for those who ask you. Even if they do not ask you, you must do it silently in your heart to God. He is the one Who can and is able to help. Be not wise in your own understanding brethren, but give place to God for it is He that is well able to do all things for their good and yours. Remember that faith is a work in one's heart, and without faith no one can please God.

Mathias had taken Luke with him earlier to milk and to draw water for our small herd of cattle. I suggested that Asher allow Astoria and I to collect the morning manna. He started to protest against it because of my injuries from the day before, but I convinced him that walking and bending would ease my sore muscles. Finally he consented. Asher's head wound was not as bad as it appeared yesterday when the blood streamed down his neck. He seemed no worse as the night wore on. Prayerfully, he will recover very nicely. My own injuries were more of an inconvenience than anything else, and I was anxious to see how Jillian and her family were doing.

We had established a bond, Jillian and I, and were making plans to spend more time together. A man can be a good, loving husband, a good friend, a good provider, a good teacher, and a good counselor all rolled up into one bundle, but there is still a cord that does not quite make a connection with his wife's thoughts and emotional understanding. It is not a bad thing but is certainly true. Most women can find that sense of understanding through friendships and trusted conversations with other women no matter the social status of each woman. Certainly, there are differences between the women according to each woman's custom, upbringing, family relations, and so forth. But there remains one common thread in females which links us in a kinship that no man can pattern. I felt that Jillian and I were destined to be good friends and companions for a long time.

****

As I began grinding the manna into the flour, I saw Jillian step out of her tent and wave. She pointed toward the inside of her tent, letting me know they were fine. I smiled, waved back to her, and continued with my work.

"Thank You, dear Lord, for Your mercy and kindness in sparing Jillian and her family," I prayed.

Reaching for a bowl, I began stirring milk into the flour. A ram's horn sounded off in the distance causing me to almost drop the bowl in my hands. Before Moses returned, there had been many horns blown and flutes with sordid music. Now since Moses was back, the horn was not for playing foolishly anymore. Asher and Mathias hurried back to inform me there was a call for all Israel to gather themselves before Moses. There was still the morning meal to be eaten and the baby to be fed. I asked Asher if he could serve himself and the children while I tended Andrew. We quickly finished eating, and he combed the children's hair while I fed the baby. Mathias covered the leftover bread and the milk jug. Then we left to join the others before Moses.

After we arrived to hear what Moses had to say, he still waited for some time until all the people were present before he began speaking.

"You have sinned this great sin, and now I will go up to the Lord. Perhaps He may forgive your transgressions," Moses told us all. Then he turned and simply walked away in the direction of the mount of God.

No one made a move to walk away or to follow behind Moses as he returned to the mountain. The sound of silence in the presence of so many people is a frightening sound to hear. The people's hearts and minds were stirred, as was mine. This was surely a time for prayer, a time for heaping hot coals of shame on our own heads, a time for falling on our knees in humility, and a time for repentance. Who knows but that God might turn and forgive our trespasses? Or that He may not? Where is the hope for us in what Moses said? What was there to hold onto in those few words he spoke? Have we come so far, and yet shall we be turned away or worse? Shall there be more punishment to come? Does Moses carry enough favor with God to persuade Him to forgive us? Has Moses enough love for Israel in his heart to even want to help us now? What are we to do now that Moses is gone once again? Will the people slide back to their wicked ways as before? Have we lost the promise of God and cast His precious gift down by the wayside? Will we live through this time of disobedience? Will we see our children grow up, or is this the last day for holding them in our arms?

If only the people standing there that day had known that God Himself was hurting, and it is not His desire to enjoy punishment at anytime. How could we have known such truths as this? How can one learn unless they are taught?

How can one be taught unless there is a preacher or a teacher? God knows all of this, and that is why He wrote the ordinances and principles on tablets. He gives gifts such as preachers and teachers and others which are anointed to understand and teach these very things. He wants us to learn about Him. No man can have such understanding about God lest he come to God and hunger to eat the bread of God's Word daily.

If God sees that a person hungers for understanding, he will surely feed understanding to him. If one hungers for wisdom, God will give that one wisdom. There is no lack in God's understanding or in His kindness. Draw close to the Lord, and He will draw close to you.

The people continued to watch Moses until he was out of sight. Now everyone felt helpless and undone. But Moses left us with a clue and being wise to pursue it would be very beneficial. Moses went to God to pray for us. This is the clue. In like manner, we must all pray for ourselves, others, and for Moses.

"If My people who are called by My name would humble themselves, pray, and turn from their wicked ways, then I would hear their prayer and turn and heal their land. O Israel, how long have I held out my arms to shelter you as a mother hen shelters her chicks beneath her wings, but you would not?" thus says the Lord God.

Someone finally broke the silence with a sound of mourning. Others listened a few moments before they, too, began to moan and be ashamed of their previous actions. Soon a few more joined in, beating their chest with their fist while looking up at the mountain. They began crying out in repentance. Many of the people quietly slipped away from the gathering, returning to the privacy of their own tents to pray. It makes no difference to God where you are or what physical position you are in at the time. Prayer is not limited to any one of these. If you have a need to pray (and we all should and must), then do so with everything in your being. Be a soldier who has a battle station under his watch; that soldier allows no ease from his insistent prayer until he sees the victory or has promise of victory in his heart.

Do not think God is deaf and needs loud prayers, and do not think He is nervous so that one must whisper to Him. God knows your station in life, and, if that is so, He will appoint seasons of prayer designed for you and will call that prayer out from you in whatever manner He desires; whether it is loud prayers or whether it be soft, gentle, whispered prayers. You must be at your station in battle gear and ready to do His will, lest you be passed by for another who will obey.

If the enemy is attacking you and your family, will you not go out to meet him? Will you cast aside your God given armor and run away? Is the battle not the Lord's, and you are His servant?

Does the soldier wield his sword for nothing? If the armor is too short, and you have need for more, will you not return to God's armory? He will supply you with what you need to fight the good fight.

If there are rocks or debris along your path of attack, will you not kick them aside so you will not fall? Will you bow before the enemy of your soul and sustain the blows he inflicts on you and not lift up a shield to protect yourself? The battleground is always in prayer, and prayer commences the moment you approach it.

Asher took my hand, and we turned to leave. My thoughts had been a whirlwind of emotional ups and downs. The experience of it all had caused a longing to be next to Moses in God's presence, praying for our people and begging for His mercy on us.

There is no distance in prayer, I thought. God knows the very thoughts and intents of the heart. It is about time we all learned that very thing.

"Hold up there a minute," Mathias called out as we were leaving for home.

He had stood beside Elder Jarrod during Moses' small speech and made his way toward us. As he came beside us, I could see in his eyes a sign of exhaustion. I had been worried about our dear friend for several days but was unwilling to say so.

The last few weeks' events had taken a toll on his old frame, yet he remained as strong as an ox. There seemed to be no time to pull up and rest since we all had a lot of thinking and planning to do concerning the situation at hand.

As we walked along, Mathias confessed what Elder Jarrod informed him about concerning yesterday's events.

He lowered his voice so others would not overhear his news, saying, "Yesterday when the Levites came with their swords to Elder Jarrod's dwelling, they killed the man who had attacked you, Leeanna."

I quickly dropped my head down and said nothing.

"It is obvious from your reaction that this news does not please you, dear woman, and God be praised that you have such a heart full of kindness. It is true that all people in their life will, and do, make bad choices and many mistakes, but God is the One Who has appointed each one's last breath to be drawn. You may be able to take some small comfort in this truth. Remember, God looks on our hearts and is not so much impressed with our actions. His righteous justice goes forth by His own wisdom, when, where, and how He chooses."

Looking up at Mathias, I managed a weak smile and thanked him for his words of comfort. Even though the man who attacked me was a mean, hateful man, he was still a human being trapped inside of a body that God's light had not been allowed to penetrate. He had seen all the wonderful things God had done for us just as all the people had, but he had hardened his own heart toward God while he partook of God's benevolence toward the people. God had examined the man's heart and found it lacking any traces of belief and change, just as He does with everyone.

God had given so many proofs of Himself to us all, yet many people had no intention of becoming one of God's own. God gave them chance after chance to see and believe. No one knows the day their life will be called out from them. Today, if you hear the Lord's voice in your heart, spirit, and soul, do not harden your heart against Him and turn away. You never know if another day will come, and you will be lost for eternity.

The wheat and tares grow together in the field of people across the earth. They all receive God's graces in the sunshine He sends, the rain He sends, and they are all nourished alike. But one day He will send His angels to harvest His field with a sharp sickle. His wheat will then be sent to heaven, but the tares will be destroyed. His sun rises and sets on the good and the evil people alike, and He knows who belongs to Him.

****

Moses and Joshua ascended the mount of God once again, but this time was a time of great sorrow and grieving for the man, Moses. With each step he took on their climb, he searched his heart for the words to pray before his Mighty God. Having been in God's presence for forty days previously, he looked forward to this time. There are no words of description, which can be told, that would clearly give one an understanding about the glorious feeling of being in God's magnificent presence. One would just have to experience that for themselves. His tired body and mind, along with his aching heart, was looking forward to the glory and love he had experienced previously.

There had been little time for Moses to commune with Joshua concerning what had taken place while he was with God. The havoc and corruption God had informed Moses about prior to his departure from Gods presence had consumed his thoughts as he and Joshua descended the mount yesterday. His faithful friend and helper, Joshua, climbed a few steps at the time before reaching back and assisting him. Joshua seemed to never tire of the old man's company, and Moses was thankful to him and to God for the young man. In past times, Moses had been diligent to repeat all the words of God in Joshua's hearing, and he was indeed aware that Joshua was in training to become a great man of God in his own time. Joshua knew his mentor was anguished in his heart and mind. So he kept his questions to himself as the two of them climbed higher and higher up the mountain.

The scene that unfolded before them as they descended this mountain yesterday had been a scene of sick depravity. He felt in his own heart a sense of utter disgust and shame when he laid eyes on that despicable golden bull Aaron had fashioned. The people who worshipped before the thing were writhing and dancing with all manner of shameful things going on. Joshua's heart had gone out to his leader, Moses, because he knew the love and hope Moses had for the people of Israel. Moses' own brother had failed to keep his commission to watch over the people and be their shepherd until Moses returned. The lie Aaron had answered Moses' question with was an unbelievable thing to hear.

Joshua noticed the trembling in Moses' hand when he reached back to assist him. Moses' age of eighty some years prevented him from being as spry as Joshua, but the older man's strength of heart could stand against the strength of all the strong men in Israel. Moses talked to God face to face and was well taught by Him, yet Moses was a very humble man and saw his relationship with God as a strong, loving, blessing.

It was evident that from the time Moses was a baby until he was turned over to Pharaoh's daughter, Moses' parents taught him about God, and was nursed from the breast of a God-fearing woman. After he was grown, even living in Pharaoh's court, the day came when Moses heard the call of God on his life, and he accepted and followed that call faithfully.

Moses had taken refuge in Midian to escape death from Pharaoh for killing an Egyptian task master whom Moses had observed beating one of his people. Over forty years spent in the backside of the wilderness tending sheep had given him time for the ways and attitudes of Egypt to be burned out of his character such as tares are of no use and are burned in the fire. After God saw that Moses had become a vessel He could mold and shape for His glory, He called him from a burning bush whose fire did not consume the bush. This understanding has a deep meaning. The burning bush shows how God can and will use willing people for His service, yet His fire brings holiness and discards the chaff without bringing destruction to the vessel.

As before, when Moses and Joshua reached a certain place on the mountain, Moses instructed Joshua to remain there as he continued up into God's presence. Waiting in the same place as before, Joshua had time to think, pray, and plan his life's work in the glory which began surrounding him. This was the life he wanted for himself and his family: to do God's work, to be a minister for God to the nation of Israel, to hear, and follow God all the days of his life. There was no other choice for him to make. This was the best choice anyone could ever make. You could give him the world and all it offered, but he would cast it far from him for only a few moments in God's presence. And to hear God say at the end of his days, "Well done, My good and faithful servant. Enter now into God's rest."

When Moses reached the top of the mountain and entered God's presence, he removed the shoes from his feet as God informed him to do. The ground he stood on was holy ground. All the words rehearsed in his heart as he climbed, fell from his memory as he knelt before that glorious wonderful Presence.

Overwhelming sorrow and heart wrenching sobs took control of his very being. Soon, he simply spread himself out on his belly before the Lord as the impact of what Israel had done flooded his heart with grief. By the kindness of the Lord, Moses was allowed a long time of preparing his heart before God. There are many weeds in the garden of our heart, and God will allow ample time for us to become aware of these weeds as we kneel before Him. He does this in order to prepare our heart to receive His divine instruction just as a farmer prepares the ground to receive the seed he sows.

"I beseech and seek You, O Lord God, truly these people have sinned a great sin and have made for themselves a god of gold. But now, if You will, forgive their sins. If You will not, blot me, I pray You, out of Your book which You have written," Moses prayed with all that was in him. His heart was truly broken before the Lord, and his passionate prayer brought a response from his Lord.

And the Lord said to Moses, "Whosoever has sinned against Me, him will I blot out of My book. Therefore now go; lead the people to the place where I tell you; Behold, My angel shall go before you, nevertheless in the day when I punish, I will visit their sin upon them. And the Lord said to Moses, "Depart and go from here to the land, you and the people whom you have brought up out of the land of Egypt. The land which I swore to Abraham, Isaac, and Jacob, saying I will give the land to your descendants. And I will send an angel before you, and he will destroy your enemies. Go to a land flowing with milk and honey. For I will not go up among you, lest I consume you along the way, for you are a stiff necked people."

Moses and Joshua returned to the camp of Israel, and an assembly of the people was called once again. When all had gathered before him, he told them what the Lord said concerning them.

The people, on hearing the news, began to mourn, and the Lord said to Moses, "Say to the children of Israel, you are a stiff necked people; I will come up among you in a moment and consume you; therefore take off your armor from you, that I may know what to do to you."

And the children of Israel stripped themselves of their armor by Mt. Horeb. Everyone who comes to God can expect to be stripped of their pride, their high thoughts, and their self-indulgence. No such weapons as these shall stand before the Lord God Almighty.

Chapter 18

Moses took his tent and set it up outside the camp and called it "the tabernacle of the congregation." As the days went on, everyone who sought to inquire of the Lord went out to the tabernacle of the congregation. This signifying that relationship with God is a personal relationship, and you must seek God from your own heart, not relying on others to do this for you. You have the personal responsibility to nurture that relationship and cannot blame others for your lack to keep it strong and healthy. Eat God's bread from your own table and be satisfied. The crumbs of bread from another's table are not as sweet as from your own.

When Moses, went out to the tabernacle, the pillar of cloud would descend and stand at the door of the tent. God would talk face to face with Moses. All of the people would stand and watch from their tent door until Moses had gone into the tent. Then the cloud descended, and they would worship the Lord. Moses would later return to the camp, but Joshua, the son of Nun, did not depart from the tabernacle. During Moses' times of communing with God before the door of the tabernacle, the Lord agreed to do as Moses prayed and go with the children of Israel on their journey.

The Lord commanded Moses to hew two stone tablets like the first ones, and write on the tablets all the words that were on the first tablets which he had broken. Moses was to be ready the next morning, and he alone would ascend the mountain again to present himself before the Lord.

During the time of all these happenings, the people began to be rooted in following God and His servant, Moses. There came a welcome change into the camp as people were starting to adhere to more teaching.

Mathias and Asher had done their share of reaching the younger men, and Elder Jarrod had taken on a great group of older men. The entire congregation of people waited patiently for Moses to return this time.

The manna continued to appear each day, and the quail continued to appear each evening. The water continued to flow, and the word of the Lord became primary in our everyday lives.

While Moses was upon the mountain another forty days and forty nights, he wrote upon the tablets the words of the covenant that God had made with Moses and Israel, the Ten Commandments.

****

As Moses approached the camp, his heart was in a state of dread. His eyes searched here and there to see if there was anything out of order or if the multitude of people had diminished in number or perhaps there might be none left here at all to greet him. The time Moses spent with God was a time of listening to all the ordinances He instructed Moses to write for the people to learn and live by. These ordinances were very significant and had purposeful meanings attached to each one. No one completely understood all the reasons and meanings for them, but they were beautiful and crucial to our way of life in becoming a holy nation of people, investing our lives in the one true God.

Moses was not aware that the skin of his face shone with a dazzling brightness from being in Gods presence. Aaron and all the people were afraid to come near him. Moses called to Aaron and all the leaders of the congregation, and they returned to him and he talked to them. Then the entire congregation returned to Moses, and he gave them in commandment all the words the Lord had given to him on Mount Sinai. (Mt. Horeb) When Moses finished speaking with us, he put a veil upon his face to cover the brightness because the people continued to stare at him in wonder.

A servant of God does not seek any glory or must not give any impression that he himself is anything. A shining face would cause the people's eyes to be on the man rather than on God. You must never follow a person because he or she has a certain gift, look, thought, talent, or charm, because they are only a human being. Whatever gift, talent, or anything else they may have is only a gift given by God, and you would make an idol for yourself by following the man, woman, or gift and not your God. This is why Moses was called "a servant of God" because his passion was for "Gods glory," and not his own glory.

But when Moses went in before the Lord, he would remove the veil from off his face, and the Lord would talk with him. He would put the veil back on his face when he came out and spoke with the children of Israel that which he was commanded. You cannot, nor will not, be able to veil your own face before the Lord for He sees all. An unveiled face represents openness in the heart to God. A veil could be a number of things you may have hidden within. It does not necessarily mean an article of clothing. A veil is anything of a veiled nature about you, but it is still seen by God and can't be hidden.

Moses spoke to us about building a tabernacle for the Presence of God to reside in as we travel toward the Promised Land. He made inquiry as to certain articles anyone may willingly give to prepare for the building of the tabernacle, the furnishings, and the garments for Aaron the high priest, and Aaron's sons the priests. The whole congregation of the children of Israel brought offerings for the Tabernacle of the Lord, for all its services, and for all the holy vestments.

****

What a grand day this has been! The entire camp has gone into a whirl of excitement on hearing the news that we, all together, have a part in giving something of our own to the Lord for a tabernacle to be constructed so that His Presence can reside here among us. Give God something of our own? Give to God? A portion of what we have will become a residence for God? Could it be that my cloth could become a curtain in His dwelling, or perhaps my gold will be melted together with other's gold and become a vessel for the service of God? Does not God own the cattle on a thousand hills and has no need to ask anyone for anything? Yet He has asked us to bring something of value from among our own possessions to use for His dwelling. This means I will have an investment in God's habitation because of a willing heart, in that future tabernacle that God looks on everyday. God looks not on the outward appearance of any man or woman, but He looks on their hearts. A willing and obedient heart are more valuable than all your gold, and with your heart invested in God, the return He gives is enormous and for an eternity.

Everyone returned to their tents and began frantically searching through their belongings to determine what could be of use for the tabernacle. Soon, people streamed toward the place where we had been instructed to bring our offerings. Baskets were fully laden with all manner of items such as gold, silver, brass, fine linen cloths, jewelry, goat's hair, red skins of rams, shittim wood, jewels, onyx stones, precious stones, spices, and oil. The number of baskets continued to mount daily until there was more than they needed and some left over. Moses had to give command not to bring anymore. The workmen sorted the items, and having received an anointing from the Lord to do all manner of skilled work, they began putting their hands to the work of the Tabernacle of the Lord.

And it came to pass, in the first month of the second year since our departure from Egypt, all the work for the tabernacle of the Lord was completed, and the tabernacle was set up on the first day of the week. Following the commandments of the Lord, all the various consecrations were performed concerning the tabernacle, Aaron, and the Levites, the sons of Aaron.

Then a cloud covered the tent of the congregation, and Moses was not able to enter the tent of the congregation because the cloud abode upon it. The glory of the Lord filled the Tabernacle of the Lord. When the cloud was lifted up from the tabernacle, the people would travel on in their journey, but if the cloud was not lifted up, they did not journey until the day it was lifted up.

"The cloud of the Lord was upon the tabernacle by day, and the pillar of fire was on it by night in the sight of all the house of Israel throughout all their journeys. God was abiding with His people, the children of Israel." (Ex: 35 – Ex: 40)

Walking in the coolness of the evening among the camps, I could not help but be fascinated at the glory the pillar of fire cast over the Tabernacle. The amber light gave not only the knowledge that our God was resident with Israel, but also provided ample light for illuminating the vast area of the camps. The security of knowing that Israel was underneath the protection of God Almighty gave us complete comfort. There was no anguish concerning enemy attacks suddenly coming upon us while we slept peacefully through the night.

I had visited the perimeter of the tent of the congregation in days past to worship God and to seek Him for direction on specific things, but now Israel's approach had an entirely different manner since the completion of The Tabernacle of the Lord. The individual rituals for different causes in seeking God's mercy, His grace, or His forgiveness was given to us by the mouth of Moses and was sustained by the work of Aaron and his sons. Because of these rituals, Israel was beginning to understand the full impact that sin brought upon us as individuals and as a nation.

To learn about the evil which dwells in one's own heart is a devastating realization. We were becoming a people of personal cleansing, beginning a different journey from inside our own hearts, and eventually culminating into personal holiness. This journey each of us must take, beginning from our own hearts, is not a pleasant one for sure. But God is faithful, and His gentle persuasion will demand this very thing from everyone who approaches Him. You cannot serve two masters. You must deprive one or the other from your heart. The choice is always your own to make. God will not share His throne with anyone, not even you.

Asher and I had begun a pattern of taking evening strolls and enjoying the peace which emanated throughout the camps. The subtle quietness of a happy and peaceful congregation had finally taken shape and was a welcome change for the entire congregation of Israel. People continued their lives with a certain awesome respect for each other because of the visible representation of God's presence among us. Of course being human beings, there were still arguments and a few fights, but the general persona of well being was tended more toward being committed to attaining peaceful results.

Acknowledging to one's self the painful truth of being two-faced in your personality is a bitter tonic to swallow. Every person alive has at one time or another experienced their own heart deceiving them and falling prey to its cunning abilities to make a wrong thing seem right in their own eyes. But such is the lesson we all must strain to learn if we are to grow healthy attitudes. We are learning that to shed one's outer skin when the inner man has become too big to contain the new self, is like a snake shedding his old skin because of its restrictions and is rewarded with another, time and again. The process can be a long and slow one indeed.

****

The intense lesson of doing things God's way and respecting His holiness came on the eighth day after the Tabernacle of the Lord had been set up. Moses directed Aaron and his sons in presenting before the Lord each separate offering, the sin offering, the burnt offering, and the peace offering. Aaron had lifted his hands and pronounced blessings upon all the people. When he came down from the offerings, he and Moses went into the tent of the congregation, came out, and blessed the people. The glory of the Lord appeared in the presence of all the people.

There came a fire out from the Lord and consumed the burnt offering and the fat upon the altar which all the people saw. They gave praise and fell on their faces before the Lord. Nadab and Abihu,

Aarons' two sons, took the golden censors, laid fire in them with incense on it, and offered it before the Lord which was not at its appointed time and not as Moses had commanded them. Fire went out from before the Lord and devoured both of them, Nadab and his brother Abihu. They died before the Lord.

Then Moses said to Aaron, "This is what the Lord has spoken saying, "I will be sanctified by those who come near Me, and before all the people I will be glorified."

And Aaron said not a word in response but held his peace. All the people saw these things happen, and the fear of the Lord came upon them. It is a true saying that the fear of the Lord is the beginning of wisdom. Our ways are not Gods ways, and our thoughts are not His thoughts.

The Lord, Himself, spoke to Aaron following this thing and told Aaron, "Do not drink wine or strong drink, neither you nor your sons with you, when you go into the tabernacle of the congregation lest you die. It shall be a statute forever throughout your generations that you may make a distinction between holy and unholy and between clean and unclean. And that you may teach the children of Israel all the statutes which the Lord has spoken to them by the hand of Moses."

Moses began to search diligently for the goat of the sin offering and found that it was burned.

He was angry with the sons of Aaron that were left, and he said to them, "Why have you not eaten the sin offering? For it is most holy and was given to you to bear the iniquity of the congregation and to make atonement for them before the Lord. Neither was the blood brought into the sanctuary as you were commanded."

Aaron said to Moses, "This day, they have offered their sin offerings and their burnt offerings before the Lord, (meaning his two sons lives having been consumed because of their sinful deed with the censors), and such things have befallen me. If I had eaten the sin offering today, would it have been better accepted in the presence of the Lord?"

When Moses heard what his brother Aaron said, he was content. Moses understood his brother's truthful reply and his heart, and he said no more about it.

****

Aaron's grief at losing two of his sons was excruciating and strength to continue on with the remains of the day was beginning to weaken. His anger fractured and ran in many different directions as the hours passed. His mind searched all avenues possible to explain to his aching heart why this thing had taken place. Aaron had learned a very expensive lesson, and the thought of arising each day to continue his duties was a hard expectation to realize. Each time his thoughts turned toward his sons, a new wave of pain assaulted his heart, and anger threatened to take him over. He was certainly learning that God was not playing games or trying to win favors, but that He is truly a living breathing God Whose love is displayed in many unsearchable ways.

Aaron knew that his wife, the mother of his sons, had been present just as all Israel had when their two sons were struck down before the Lord. His heart ached to be with her at this time so they could comfort each other, but it was not possible for him to leave his station until all his duties were completed. He also could be struck down, and his wife would be left a widow if that were to happen. His mind raced back to the day Moses had returned from the mountain and found the golden calf. Why was I spared from sure destruction? Had my sin not been as great as my now deceased sons? He had lain awake at night wondering when punishment would come on his head. If indeed he had died that very day Moses discovered the calf, his pain would have been less severe, he thought, than what he was experiencing now. Aaron tried to clear his mind from such thoughts, but like a thorn in his side, they continued to prick his mind.

Aaron was not alone in grieving over lost loved ones. It was not foreign to hear occasional burst of crying coming from the tents of some left as widows, sisters, daughters, or brides to be, for their loved ones who fell by the sword of the Levites. Trying to bring words of comfort to those who were hurting was a sensitive job indeed. What could one say that would bring such words of comfort? How could one respond to their questions of why did this happen? A shoulder to cry on or a hug as they cried until their eyes were swollen was about the only thing one could feel safe in offering. No one understands the why's and how's of what God deems necessary in His wisdom. We must simply try to accept His works. That answer in itself lacks an acceptable explanation for those hurting, but it's the only answer I can give.

Now that the Tabernacle of the Lord has been completed with all that was involved, there is rumor about the camps that Israel will soon pack up and continue forward on her journey. We have abided in this same place for over a full year now and such a welcome change would be good for us all.

When God decides it is time to move forward, He will instruct Moses about His plan, and Moses will instruct the people. The cloud will lift up from the Tabernacle, and Israel will follow in God's directed path.

****

Chapter 19

" We must pack our belongings quickly," Asher told our family. "The congregation will be moving tomorrow. Everything must be tightly packed, and the tent will be the last thing to come down at daybreak. We have waited a long time here in this place, many things have happened, but I will be glad to have this place behind us."

Asher began picking at several items setting around our tent in an attempt to begin packing. I waited for a moment to allow the news to sink into my head before trying to help him with the task.

"Let me and Mathias handle the packing, Leeanna. It must be packed tightly so the loads we carry will not be so bulky," Asher said as he shooed me from the tents interior.

"At least allow me to pack little Andrew's things so I will know where to find them when needed," I responded from outside the tent.

And so it came to pass that on the twentieth day of the second month in the second year the cloud lifted up from the tabernacle. The children of Israel took their journey from the wilderness of Sinai, and the cloud rested again in the wilderness of Paran. We took our journey for the first time, went three days from the mount of God, and the Ark of the Covenant of the Lord went before us one day's journey to prepare a resting place for us.

After a brief stay at Paran, we departed by commandment of the Lord through Moses to Hazeroth and stayed there for a time. It was here that another great event happened in Israel. Aaron, and Miriam, his sister, became angry with Moses because of Moses' wife for he had married an Ethiopian woman.

They spoke against their brother Moses jealousy saying, "Indeed has the Lord only spoken by Moses? Has He not spoken by us also?"

Miriam's reward for this came in the form of leprosy on her. Be assured that God makes no mistakes in choosing persons to speak for and represent Him, and God alone had chosen Moses for this work. The key word is "God chose." There are many who set themselves in position saying they are working for God, yet it is apparent that God did not choose them. God looked on the heart of Moses. He tested Moses and found Moses passed His test. God spent days teaching and grooming him to represent His words before all Israel, and "Gods choice" was done by His own wisdom. Be careful what you say against "Gods anointed" spokesperson. There are many spokespersons, but God did not "choose" them, so curb your tongue lest you be found in a fire kindled by your own tongue. Such a mistake could be your last mistake.

By command of the Lord, Moses had appointed twelve chief men, one from each of the twelve tribes of Israel, to go over and spy out the land of Canaan that God had given to the children of Israel.

Moses commanded the twelve men to search out the land thoroughly saying, "Go up this way to the south, and go up on the mountain. See what the land is and the people who live in the land, whether they are strong or weak, few or many. Seek knowledge if the land is fertile, if the land is poor, and whether it has trees in it or not. Be of good courage, and bring some of the fruit of the land back with you." (NU. 13)

The twelve men did as they were commanded and searched out all the land, cutting down a branch with one bunch of grapes, and carried it between them on a pole. They also brought some pomegranates and figs. After forty days of spying out the land, the men returned to the camps of Israel there in the wilderness of Hazaroth. They came before Moses and the entire congregation showing them the fruit of the land.

They went to Moses and said, "We went to the land to which you sent us, and surely it flows with milk and honey, and this is the fruit of it. The land is truly great and vast with all manner of good things, but the cities are large and fortified, and the inhabitants are strong and numerous and of many different races. There are giants there great and tall, and we felt like grasshoppers in size compared to them."

The whole congregation gasped and began to murmur, shaking their heads as fear gripped their hearts with thoughts of confronting such people as these. Joshua and Caleb became alarmed at the people's reaction to this news. Waving their arms frantically in the air, the two men began to shout to their fearful brethren.

Caleb told us, "Let us go up at once and possess the land for we are well able to overcome our enemies."

The other ten men, who had gone to help spy out the land, spoke up and said, "We are not able to go up against these people for they are stronger than we! The land we went through to spy out is a land which devours its inhabitants, and all the people we saw are of great stature. We saw there giants and the sons of giants. We were to them like grasshoppers, and, in their eyes, we are as nothing."

The entire congregation was in a commotion, crying loudly. They continued to fret and cry through the night.

Many began to murmur against Moses and Aaron and the whole congregation said to them, "Would to God that we had died in the land of Egypt or that we would have died in this wilderness. Why has the Lord brought us into this land to fall by the sword, and our wives and children would be prey for our enemies. We were better off in Egypt."

The people said to one another, "Let us appoint another leader and return to Egypt."

The people's derision began to stir up thoughts of stoning Moses and Aaron as the climate of their discussions grew hot against going on with this unthinkable planned journey into the land of Canaan. What would become of this great nation of people? This Moses and his sidekick brother were surely leading us into certain death. What could they be thinking? At least we could try going back to Egypt and possibly beg their forgiveness! A land flowing with milk and honey, huh! Sounds more like a land that will be flowing with Israelite blood, and we will not stand and be slaughtered at the request of anyone. Who does he think he is, this Moses?" (NU: 14)

Immediately upon hearing this, Moses and Aaron fell with their faces toward the ground before the congregation of Israel. They began to pray fervently to the Lord on behalf of this angry mob before them. Joshua and Caleb tore their own clothes as a sign of their horror and shame against the congregations' blasphemous plans.

They said to the people, "The land we passed through to spy it out is an exceedingly good land. If the Lord delights in us, he will bring us into this land and give it to us, a land which flows indeed with milk and honey" This means a land full and abundant. "Only do not rebel against the Lord. Neither be afraid of the people of the land for their conquest will be as easy as eating bread for their strength has left them. The Lord is with us. So do not be afraid of them."

The whole congregation was set on stoning them with stones. But the glory of the Lord appeared in the cloud in the tabernacle of the congregation before all the people of Israel, and they all saw it.

The Lord said to Moses, "How long will these people provoke Me? And how long will they not believe Me for all the signs which I have done among them? I will strike them with pestilence and destroy them. I will make of you, Moses, a nation which is greater and mightier than they are."

Moses answered the Lord saying, "Then the Egyptians would hear of it and tell it to the people of the land for they have heard that You, Lord, are in the midst of this people, Israel, and that You are seen face to face. Your cloud stands over them, and You go before them in a pillar of cloud by day and a pillar of fire by night. If You kill all these people as one man, then the nations who have heard of Your fame will say, "The Lord their God was not able to bring them into the land which He promised them, therefore He has slain them in the wilderness."

Moses continued, "And now, let Your power, O Lord, be great as according to what You have spoken saying, The Lord is longsuffering and of great mercy, and will forgive iniquity and transgression, by no means clearing the guilty, but visiting the iniquity of the fathers upon the third and fourth generations of those who hate Me." Moses continued to pray saying, "Pardon the iniquity of these people according to Your great mercy as You have forgiven them from Egypt even until now."

And the Lord said to Moses, "I have forgiven them according to your word, but as truly as I live, the whole earth shall be filled with the glory of the Lord. And yet all men who have seen My glory and all the signs I performed have tempted Me ten times, and have not listened and obeyed My voice. Surely, they shall not see the land, not even one of those who have provoked Me. But My servants, Caleb and Joshua, who have followed My spirit fully, I will bring into the land, and their descendants shall possess it." (NU: 14)

The Lord continued saying to Moses, "Tomorrow turn the people and set out for the wilderness by the way of the Red Sea." Then the Lord spoke to Moses and to Aaron, saying, "How long shall this wicked congregation murmur in My presence? I have heard their complaints which they murmur in My presence." Say to them, "As I live, says the Lord, and as you have spoken in My presence, so will I do to you. Your corpses shall fall in this wilderness, those that were numbered of you, according to the whole number, from twenty years old and upward, because you have murmured against Me. You shall not come into the land of promise, but your little ones, whom you said would become the prey, they shall enter into the land, and I will bring them there, and they shall know the land which you have despised. A year for each day you spied out the land shall you wander in this wilderness, even forty years because you murmured against Me."

All ten men who had given an evil report to the people upon returning from spying out the land and caused the people to murmur against the Lord, died by a sudden plague before the Lord. But Joshua and Caleb still lived. When Moses told all of what the Lord said to him, the people mourned greatly, and rose up early the next morning and went up to the top of the mountain saying, "Look, we will go up to the place which the Lord has promised us for we have sinned."

Moses tried to convince them that they were disobeying the command of the Lord yet again, and God would not be with them if they went up there, but they would not listen and proceeded on up. The Amalekites and the Canaanites, who dwelt in that mountain, came down and killed them and pursued them as far as Hirmah. (NU: 15)

Hard and painful lessons to learn, one would say. We were beginning to understand that if you are not in God, then you are indeed on your own in this world. That mistake Israel made on that particular day was a bloody, painful one which we would never forget. Though we still have a long road ahead of us, our children will go in and possess the Promised Land. Before this generation has all died out, we will have learned that God is truly a God of His word.

My Asher fell upon that mountain that day as did so many of the brave men of Israel. Asher felt constrained to show the people and his God that to obey God was better than sacrifice, but he forgot that feelings are not necessarily the right path to follow when they are in direct conflict with what God has said. I am raising the children by myself now, and we all continue to roam through this wilderness year after year.

There is so much more to tell concerning our journey to the Promise Land. Please allow me a little time to reflect and catch my breath, but be aware that I will be faithful to tell you about this miraculous journey as my life continues. Astoria will take up where I leave off because I have invested all my memories into her for relaying them to others. May God be with us all. Amen and amen, Leeanna Asher.

Epilogue

Leeanna and the children continue forward on this miraculous journey, supported by their friends and relations. As the children grow, many events happen which are used to bring Godly teaching into their lives. Her life story will thrill, encourage, strengthen, teach, and bless you, in "The Journey Part Two". Watch the pages come alive with surprises and blessings! Keep the tissues handy.

www.ingramcontent.com/pod-product-compliance
Lightning Source LLC
Chambersburg PA
CBHW020437290526
45785CB00002B/897